BUILDING PEACE
IN HAITI

BUILDING PEACE IN HAITI

CHETAN KUMAR

LYNNE
RIENNER
PUBLISHERS

BOULDER
LONDON

Published in the United States of America in 1998 by
Lynne Rienner Publishers, Inc.
1800 30th Street, Boulder, Colorado 80301

and in the United Kingdom by
Lynne Rienner Publishers, Inc.
3 Henrietta Street, Covent Garden, London WC2E 8LU

Library of Congress Cataloging-in-Publication Data
Kumar, Chetan.
   Building peace in Haiti   /   Chetan Kumar.
   (International Peace Academy occasional paper
series)
   ISBN 1-55587-770-2 (pbk.   :   alk. paper)
   1. United Nations—Haiti.   2. National security—Haiti.
   I. Title. II. Series.
   JZ4997.5.H2K86   1998
   327.7294—dc21
                                                98-25923
                                                    CIP

British Cataloguing in Publication Data
A Cataloguing in Publication record for this book
is available from the British Library.

Printed and bound in the United States of America

⊗   The paper used in this publication meets the requirements
    of the American National Standard for Permanence of
    Paper for Printed Library Materials Z39.48-1984.

   5   4   3   2   1

CONTENTS

ACKNOWLEDGMENTS

This occasional paper is a product of the International Peace Academy (IPA) project titled "Peacebuilding: Legacies and Strategies." The research that produced this project would not have been possible without generous support from the Carnegie Corporation of New York, the Ford Foundation, and the John D. and Catherine T. MacArthur Foundation. The actual publication of this occasional paper has been made possible by a generous grant from the United States Institute for Peace.

Several IPA staff members have contributed significantly to this paper with invaluable ideas, suggestions, and advice. In particular, I wish to thank Olara A. Otunnu, who until recently served as president of IPA; Michael W. Doyle of Princeton University, member of the IPA Board of Directors; Lt.-Col. Remi Landry, senior associate for training; and Elizabeth Cousens, senior associate. Critical administrative support was provided by Florence Mussafi, senior administrative assistant, and Robert Schupp, publications coordinator.

Several individuals outside IPA also contributed greatly to this effort. A number of senior UN officials who have provided valuable advice and suggestions over the past two years must, of necessity, remain unnamed. However, I can thank H.E. Mr. Pierre Lelong, Haiti's permanent representative to the United Nations, Jocelyn McCalla of the National Coalition for Haitian Rights, and Col. J. Michael Snell of Canada's Permanent Mission to the United Nations for insights that I would otherwise have missed.

Finally, I thank my wife, Beth, for her infinite patience and care that are so essential for all such efforts.

ACRONYMS AND ABBREVIATIONS

CARICOM	Caribbean Community
CBI	Caribbean Basin Initiative
FADH	Forces Armée d'Haiti, the Haitian Armed Forces
FRAPH	Fronte Révolutionnaire pour l'Avancement et le Progrès en Haiti, a militia
HNPTC	Haitian National Police Training Center
IPSF	Interim Public Security Force
MICIVIH	International Civilian Mission in Haiti
MIPONUH	United Nations Civilian Police Mission in Haiti
MNF	Multinational Force
OPL	Originally Organisation Politique Lavalas, now Organisation du Peuple en Lutte
SRSG	Special Representative of the UN Secretary-General
UN CIVPOL	United Nations Civilian Police
UNDP	United Nations Development Program
UNMIH	United Nations Mission in Haiti
UNSMIH	United Nations Support Mission in Haiti
UNTMIH	United Nations Transition Mission in Haiti

HAITI

- –··–··– International boundary
- –·–·–·– Departmental boundary
- ⊙ National capital
- ○ Departmental seat
- ○ Town, village
- ──── Main road
- ──── Secondary road
- ✦ Airport
- ✦ Airstrip

0 5 10 15 20 25 mi
0 10 20 30 40 km

ATLANTIC OCEAN

DOMINICAN REPUBLIC

Monte Cristi

ÎLE DE LA TORTUE

Palmiste

Baie de Mancenille

Mont Organisé

Cap-Haïtien

Quartier Morin
Caracol
Phaéton
Fort-Liberté
Ferrier
Dérac

NORD-EST

Cerca-la-Source

Mont Cabao

Acul du Nord
Plaine du Nord
Limonade
Sainte-Suzanne
Grand Bassin
Trou-du-Nord
Terrier-Rouge
Dondon
Milot

Vallières

St. Louis du Nord
Anse-à-Foleur
Le Borgne
Port-Margot

Limbé
Pilate
Plaisance
Marmelade

NORD

Saint-Raphaël
Bahon
Grande Rivière du Nord
Ranquitte
La Victoire
Pignon
Crochu

Mombin-Crochu
Carice

Perches

Mont Organisé

Belladère
Baptiste
Savanette
Cornillon

Cerca
Carvajal
Maïssade

Hinche

Thomassique

Thomonde

Lac de Péligre

Mirebalais
Saut d'Eau

Belle-Anse
Bodarie
Thiotte
Banane

Anse-à-Pitres
Pedernales

NORD-OUEST

Port-de-Paix
Bassin-Bleu
Gros-Morne
Terre-Neuve

Jean-Rabel
Pointe Jean-Rabel

Môle St-Nicolas
Bombardopolis
Baie de Henne
Anse-Rouge

Cap Saint-Nicolas
Cap-à-Foux

Gonaïves

Ennery

ARTIBONITE

Saint Michel de l'Attalaye

Dessalines

Saint-Marc

Petite-Rivière de l'Artibonite
Verrettes

La Chapelle

Duvalierville

Arcahaie

Lascahobas

Saut d'Eau

Croix des Bouquets

Ganthier
Pétion-Ville

Étang Saumâtre

Fonds-Verrettes
Fond Parisien

Cornillon

Thomazeau

PORT-AU-PRINCE

Gressier
Carrefour
Léogâne

CENTRE

Pointe de Montrouis

Anse-à-Galets

Pointe Fantasque

ÎLE DE LA GONÂVE

Canal de Saint-Marc

Pointe Ouest

Pointe-à-Raquette

Golfe de la Gonâve

Canal de la Gonâve

Anse-à-Veau

Petit Trou de Nippes

PRESQU'ÎLE DES BARADÈRES

Petite Rivière de Nippes
Miragoâne
L'Asile

Baradères

Vieux Bourg d'Aquin
Aquin

Petit-Goâve
Grand-Goâve
Trouin

La Vallée de Jacmel

Côtes-de-fer

Cap Raymond

OUEST

Kenscoff
Bainet

Marigot
Cayes-Jacmel

Jacmel

Grand-Gosier

SUD-EST

CARIBBEAN SEA

ÎLE A VACHE
Baie de Jacmel

ILES CAYÉMITES

Corail
Pestel
Roseaux

Camp-Perrin

Maniche

Cavaillon
St. Louis du Sud

SUD

Chantal
Torbeck
St-Jean du Sud

Les Cayes

Jérémie

Trou Bonbon

Abricots

Moron
Chambellan
Dame-Marie
Anse d'Hainault
Les Irois

GRANDE-ANSE

Source Chaude

Coteaux
Chardonnières
Les Anglais
La Cahouane
Tiburon

Port-à-Piment
Roche-à-Bateau
Port-Salut

The boundaries and names shown on this map do not imply official endorsement or acceptance by the United Nations.

Department of Public Information
Cartographic Section

Map No. 3855 Rev. 1   UNITED NATIONS
October 1995 (Colour)

Chronology of
Key Developments

In the following chronology, facts, dates, events, and comments on the significance of certain events from the period between 1697 and the departure from Haiti of President Jean-Claude Duvalier in 1986 are drawn mainly from information provided in Michel-Rolph Trouillot, *Haiti: State Against Nation—Origins and Legacy of Duvalierism* (New York: Monthly Review, 1990). Dates and events from 1986 to the election of President Aristide in 1990 are drawn primarily from material presented in Amy Wilentz, *The Rainy Season: Haiti Since Duvalier* (New York: Touchstone Books, 1989). Dates and events from the 1990 election through the 1991 coup and the restoration of democracy in 1994 are drawn primarily from the chronology in James Ridgeway, ed., *The Haiti Files: Decoding the Crisis* (Washington, D.C.: Essential Books, 1994). Developments in Haiti following the restoration of democracy in 1994 are reported in Chapter 2 of this occasional paper.

1697   Spain acknowledged the French occupation of the Western half of the island of Hispaniola, which was thereafter known as Saint-Domingue.

1760–1790 Saint-Domingue became the leading coffee exporter in the Western world.

1791   In the summer of 1791, a series of secret religious ceremonies was conducted at Bois Cayman by the slave overseer and *voudoun* priest Boukman, in which the slaves plotted the overthrow of their masters.

1791–1804 War of independence led by Toussaint l'Ouverture.

1793   On August 29, at the Declaration of Camp Turel, slaves and freedmen, *mulâtres* and blacks alike declared their common goal to end slavery in Haiti forever.

1802   Toussaint l'Ouverture was captured and exiled to France, where he died in imprisonment.

1804   Saint-Domingue became independent as the Republic of Haiti, with Jean-Jacques Dessalines as the first president.

1804–1810   Tensions developed between members of the Haitian elite who wanted to retain plantation agriculture under Haitian leadership and the freed slaves who wanted a system of smallholder farming.[1]

1805   Dessalines, who had declared himself emperor, was killed in an ambush. He was succeeded by Alexandre Petion in 1807. Simultaneously, Henri Christophe declared a Kingdom of the North in Cap-Haitien.

1807   In March, the Haitian Senate, under General Guy-Joseph Bonnet, approved a system of taxation on agricultural products—primarily sugar and coffee—that employed customs house levies and revenue collection in kind to finance the state. Over the next century and a half, this system became the mainstay of a Haitian state through which a small, predatory elite lived off the toil of the peasants.[2]

1810   Seventy-three percent of Haitian government's revenue was collected at customs houses by this year.[3] This figure continued to rise throughout Haitian history, making customs houses an important prize for factions contending for control of the government.

1820   Haiti was reunited under President Jean-Pierre Boyer.

1825   France, under Charles X, imposed an indemnity on Haiti for the war of independence. Other European powers tacitly hinged their recognition of Haiti on the payment of this indemnity. The Haitian government, under Boyer, agreed to pay the indemnity.

1825   At the Congress of Panama of the nations of the Western Hemisphere, the United States insisted against Haiti's participation, thus creating a hemispheric embargo of Haiti. Other nations followed suit.

1826   President Boyer instituted his famous Rural Code.

1843   Hérard Dumesle, a Jeremie-based civil servant, publicly critiqued injustices committed by the government. President Boyer fired Dumesle. Senator Beaubrun Ardouin, a prominent figure of his times, publicly supported the firing. An anonymous critic responded with a tract in which he suggested that Ardouin's support implied a passive civil service with no ability to function independently. Ardouin published his own tract in which he suggested that a civil service, by its very nature, should be completely beholden to the executive. Ardouin's position, which was supported by his colleagues, set the tone for the relationship between Haiti's civil service and its rulers. Civil service appointments and firings were henceforth no longer carried out on the basis of merit, but entirely on political considerations.[4]

1843   President Jean-Pierre Boyer was overthrown in a coup, and succeeded by Charles-Rivière Herard.

1849   President Faustin Soulouque led Haiti in an attack on the eastern half of Hispaniola, thus bedevilling relations between Haiti and the Dominican Republic to this day.

1860   The Vatican recognized Haiti. The Vatican's previous lack of recognition resulted in a general disdain for Haiti and its independence by most European powers.

1862   Following the end of slavery in the United States, the American government recognized Haiti.

1876   Haitian economist Edmond Paul, in his book De l'Impôt sur le Café, detailed the extent to which taxes on the export of coffee, one of the mainstays of the Haitian state, burdened the peasantry.[5]

1890   The merchants obtained an agreement from the government to sign over to them any appreciation in coffee revenues in order to repay loans that they had provided to the state. This arrangement, one of many similar agreements throughout the nineteenth century, symbolized the constant domination of the Haitian state by the mercantile class, which lived off the value extracted from the labor of the peasantry.[6]

1890–1915   Tensions increased among Haiti's mercantile class and the ruling elite over the apportioning of spoils from a shrinking productive base. Agricultural productivity declined because the predatory elite made no investment in the factors of production.[7]

1915   President Vibrun Guillame Sam was butchered by a mob in the streets of Port-au-Prince. Three of his predecessors had also met a similar fate between 1911 and 1915. Claiming to restore stability, the United States invaded the same day, appointed Philippe-Sudre Dartiguenave president, and forced the Haitian Senate to ratify him. It then took control of Haiti's customs houses (the sustenance of the elite) and the treasury, and disbanded the Haitian army.

1917–1920   The United States attempted to force the peasantry into organized labor. Resistance to these attempts prompted a guerrilla rebellion by Charlemagne Peralte. At its height the rebellion included 15,000 peasants. U.S. Marines killed Peralte and crushed the rebellion in 1919. They then established forced labor camps in which another 5,500 peasants died.

1920–1930   The United States completed the training and installment of the Garde Nationale d'Haiti, which subsequently became notorious Forces Armée d'Haiti. The new force was created and trained for the sole purpose of internal repression.

1928   The U.S. tendency to favor lighter-colored Haitians in positions of government and power stimulated the launch of a movement of cultural revival (the *indigéniste* movement), the arrival of which was heralded by Jean-

Price Mars' book, *Ainsi parla l'oncle.*[8] While the *indigéniste* was a cultural movement, it provided the broad legitimacy for the rise of a movement for black political power, *noirisme,* on the shoulders of which François Duvalier ascended to power in the years after the U.S. departure.

1930   Dartiguenave's successor, President Stenio Vincent, began the process of negotiating an end to the U.S. presence in Haiti.

1934   U.S. Marines left Haiti.

1946   Haiti experienced a populist upsurge led by Major Paul Magloire of the new army. A series of student and street protests forced the resignation of President Elie Lescot. Major Magloire and the army organized elections in which they forced through the election of a *noiriste* (black nationalist), Dumarsais Estimé, as president.

1950   Magloire himself took over from Estimé as president. While he gave a number of *noiristes* important government positions, he did little to address the grievances of Haiti's masses.

1957   *Noiriste* leader Dr. François Duvalier was able to build enough of a relationship with the military to get himself elected as president in an election dominated by the army.

1957–1986 Under François Duvalier and his son, Jean-Claude Duvalier, Haiti experienced some of the worst repression in its history. Trouillot points out that so intense and murderous was the repression that many analysts came to see Haiti's crisis as a result of the dictatorship, instead of the dictatorship itself as having resulted from the bigger structural crisis of the complete exclusion and exploitation of the peasantry by the urban elite.[9]

1957   At the hands of officers who had graduated from the training for the new U.S.-created army in 1931, the military became a major force in politics, using gross repression and brutality as its primary political tools. The term *kansonférisme* ("iron pant" politics) became widely used in Haiti to describe the new totalitarianism.[10] The military inaugurated the Duvalier era by shutting down the media and the judiciary.

1960–1962   In keeping with the rhetoric of the *noiristes,* Duvalier targeted the French-dominated Catholic Church and expelled three of its top bishops, thus decimating the Church and making it subservient to his control.

1962   President Duvalier created the dreaded militia known as Volunteers for National Security (VSN), or *tonton macoutes.* Instead of modeling the VSN as a praetorian guard, he recruited VSN members from all parts of the bourgeoisie, thus creating a national network of patronage and terror held together as much by rumor and suspicion as personal loyalty to the president.

1962   In return for voting for the expulsion of Cuba from the Organization of American States, Duvalier was able to obtain U.S. financing for the building of the François Duvalier International Airport.

1963   François Duvalier finished consolidating his control of the army by exploiting divisions of class and color in the armed forces. While he promoted black officers from the lower ranks, between 1957 and 1963 he exiled three successive chiefs of staff and made the office of chief of staff an irrelevant appendage of the presidency.

1967   Though *noiriste* ideology targeted Haiti's mercantile elite and some prominent members of the *mulâtre* elite were expelled, merchants' profits actually grew under Duvalier. This was the price paid to keep them out of politics. Trouillot points out that by 1967, merchants were appropriating nearly 60 percent of all proceeds from the sale of agricultural produce.[11]

1969   After brutally persecuting Haitian intellectuals for several years in the name of fighting Communism, Duvalier instituted a draconian Anti-Communist Law, partly to establish his *bona fides* with the United States.

1969   U.S. Vice-President Nelson Rockefeller rewarded

Duvalier's anti-Communist zeal with a visit, during which Duvalier predicted that Haiti was an ideal location for businessmen seeking offshore assembly platforms.

1971   François Duvalier died and was succeeded by his son Jean-Claude Duvalier. The *noiriste* presidencies of Estimé, Magloire, and Duvalier had not only not produced any relief for Haiti's largely black masses, the latter's condition had actually worsened. This demonstrated that the primary political dynamic in Haiti was not that of color but of class.[12]

1971   President Jean-Claude Duvalier put forward *Jean-Claudisme*—a loose amalgam of ideas aimed at industrializing Haiti through assembly manufacturing, developed with the help of international donors and the Haitian elite—to replace *noirisme* as the dominant state ideology.

1971   Electricité d'Haiti began operating as the new national public utility with the inauguration of a hydroelectric plant at Péligre.

1980   President Jean-Claude Duvalier married Michele Bennett, a member of the *mulatre* elite, to formally indicate his willingness to work with the elite instead of having an acrimonious relationship with them like his father had.

1982   On September 12, a young priest named Jean-Bertrand Aristide, shortly after being ordained, preached a sermon in which he denounced the Duvaliers and the misery of Haiti's masses.

1970–1985   Largely as a result of attempts to develop Haiti as an offshore assembly platform, Haiti's dependence on imported food, as well as food prices, rose exponentially.

1983   In a visit to Haiti in 1983, Pope John Paul II endorsed the work of the Haitian Catholic Church in spreading a message of social justice among Haiti's poor.

1984   Popular demonstrations began on a large scale, inspired by the rise in food prices, the influx of unemployed labor from rural areas, and the preaching of liberation theology priests. Initially targeted against poverty, they soon became an outcry against the Duvalier regime.

1985   According to U.S. press reports of the time, Michele Bennett-Duvalier, in an act reminiscent of Marie Antoinette, spent U.S. $ 1.7 million on a two-week trip to Paris.

1985   The government's brutal attempts to suppress protest peaked with the massacre of four schoolchildren in Gonaives on November 27. The United States publicly distanced itself from its client.

1986   On February 7, President Jean-Claude Duvalier and his wife went into exile on an American military plane. The United States helped to engineer a transitional government headed by Brigadier-General Henri Namphy, which declared an overall agenda of holding democratic elections and continuing the U.S.-favored strategy of promoting assembly manufacturing.

1986   The period immediately after the Duvaliers' departure was followed by a mob vendetta against some members of the *tonton macoutes*. Known as the *dechoukaj*, this vendetta targeted only some of the lower ranks of the former VSN, and as with everything else in Haiti, left the overall structure of exploitation intact.[13]

1987   On November 7, some 200,000 Haitians took to the streets of Port-au-Prince to protest the disappearance at the hands of the military of Charlot Jacquelin, a worker for a Catholic charity known as Mission Alpha. Jacquelin's disappearance and the ensuing events signified that the departure of the Duvaliers was a relatively insignificant episode in what had become a vast struggle by the majority of Haitians for basic rights. In fact, in its brief years in power the Namphy junta abducted and slaughtered more Haitians than Jean-Claude Duvalier had in his fifteen years.[14]

1987   At the end of January, the first National Congress of Democratic Movements brought a large number of

Haitian prodemocracy organizations to reconcile different sectors in creating a common strategy for democracy. This was the first such event of its kind in Haitian history.

1987   On March 29, Haitians overwhelmingly approved a Constitution written by a Constituent Assembly appointed by the military. In order to generate public enthusiasm, the Assembly included a provision to ban Duvalierists from politics for the next ten years. It also called for elections in the fall of 1987. Many considered the whole exercise a sham since the junta could not be expected to let a truly representative government be formed.

1987   On July 23, army- and landowner-backed thugs hacked to death several hundred peasants participating in a land reform program in Jean-Rabel, in the famished Northwest, and scattered their bodies in nearby ravines. Despite this massacre, the international community remained resolute in its belief in the junta's ability to hold free and fair elections.

1987   Soldiers in uniform, together with former *macoutes*, brutally massacred voters by the dozens as they lined up at schools and town halls to vote in the November elections. The junta feared that Gerard Gorgue, candidate of the Unity Front—a coalition of prodemocracy organizations—might win. Having dispersed the voters, the junta then cancelled the elections and dismissed the Provisional Electoral Council charged with conducting the elections.

1988   On January 18, 1988, the junta organized a sham election under a puppet electoral council. They then handed the elections on a platter to Leslie Manigat, the candidate with whom they felt most comfortable. Manigat then tried to control the army by dismissing and replacing some top officers, including Namphy. On June 19, the army dismissed him and restored Namphy as president.

1988   Through the summer of 1988, the army widened its attacks on nascent peasant organizations by targeting Chavannes Jean-Baptiste's Hinche-based Mouvman

Papaye Paysan, one of the country's largest peasant movements.

1988   On September 11, army thugs invaded Aristide's church, St. Jean Bosco, while he was delivering mass, and slaughtered thirteen people, critically wounding seventy-seven others. Aristide himself barely escaped, along with peasant leader Chavannes Jean-Baptiste, who was also present.

1988   On September 18, Gen. Prosper Avril eased Namphy out of power and became president. The United States reportedly eased the transition. While the new Avril government lacked the gratuitously brutal approach of the previous regime, it did not undertake any policies aimed at relieving the suffering of Haiti's masses. In accordance with U.S. wishes, however, Avril promised democratic elections.

1990   Democratic elections were finally held in December under the transitional government of Ertha Pascal-Trouillot, who had taken over from Avril. The army was restrained by the large presence of international monitors, and by the fact that the U.S.-backed candidate Marc Bazin was expected to win. Surprisingly, Father Aristide won, after a last-minute candidacy on the platform of the FNCD coalition. Aristide was recognized as the national leader of a broad network of prodemocracy, grassroots organizations that he called the Lavalas ("flood") movement.

1991   Roger LaFontant, former head of the dreaded VSN, attempted a coup prior to Aristide's inauguration on January 7. Immediate popular reaction, together with complete lack of international support, quickly aborted the coup.

1991   Between January and September, Aristide attempted to push through progressive legislation to streamline the economy, improve tax collection, and reform agriculture. Most legislation was blocked by the parliament, which still consisted largely of representatives of traditional political organizations and not Lavalas activists.

1991   On September 27, President Aristide called for the elite to join a national effort of reform and renewal. He also reportedly urged the masses to resort to harsher measures if the popular will was thwarted.

1991   The military overthrew the president on September 30. Aristide was allowed to escape to Venezuela. The military immediately launched an attack against Aristide supporters, slaughtering more than a thousand in the next two weeks. Some 200,000 people fled the capital in response to this repression.

1991   An OAS mission visited Haiti on October 5, only to be roughed up by the military. Two days later, the OAS voted to impose a comprehensive embargo against the military government. The UN General Assembly condemned the coup on October 11 and deemed the regime illegal. On November 5, the United States imposed an embargo on all commercial traffic to and from Haiti. A second OAS mission returned in November under Augusto Ocampo, but met only with members of the army and the business and political elite.

1992   In January, under an OAS plan in which he would return to Haiti with a new prime minister and a group of OAS monitors, Aristide agreed to appoint Rene Theodore, a former opponent, as prime minister. Theodore's choice was supported by the new pro-coup leadership of the parliament.

1992   By February, a flood of refugees had already started to flee the brutality of the government. Sixteen thousand people had already been picked up by the U.S. Coast Guard, while many others had perished at sea.

1992   On February 23, an OAS-mediated accord was signed in Washington under which the coup plotters would be granted amnesty, legislation enacted by the parliament after the coup would be considered legal, and no firm date would be set for President Aristide's return, even though Rene Theodore would become prime minister.

1992   The State Department declared on February 25 that
            Ambassador Adams would work towards creating a gov-
            ernment of consensus in Haiti.

1992   On March 27, the Haitian Supreme Court rejected the
            Washington accord as unconstitutional. Cedras and the
            Senate both rejected the accord in April, demonstrating
            that the military was unwilling to allow Aristide's
            return.

1992   On May 8, the army, the executive installed by the army
            (President Nerette and Prime Minister Honorat), and
            the Parliament signed the Villa d'Accueil accord which
            called for a government of "consensus."

1992   On May 24, President George Bush signed an executive
            order declaring that all Haitians caught trying to enter
            the United States on boats would immediately be sent
            back to Haiti without any attempts to determine whether
            they had any legitimate claims to asylum.

1992   On June 4, Marc Bazin became prime minister of Haiti
            under the Villa d'Accueil accord.

1992   On September 16, an OAS civilian monitoring mission
            arrived in Haiti. They were confined to their hotel for
            several months.

1992   In November, the military killed two members of KON-
            AKOM, the pro-Aristide party of Victor Benoit—just one
            of the many killings of journalists, activists, and common
            persons suspected of having pro-Aristide or prodemocra-
            cy tendencies during 1992. Other victims included
            George Izmery, brother of pro-Aristide businessman
            Antoine Izmery.

1992   On December 23, Marc Bazin issued a call to negotiate
            with Aristide.

1993   Going back on his campaign promises, President Clinton
            announced in January that he would continue the policy
            of interdicting Haitian refugees at sea and returning

them to Haiti. The same month, the army conducted fake elections in order to further alter the composition of the Senate in its favor.

1993   The United Nations appointed Dante Caputo as a joint UN/OAS envoy to Haiti, to take over from Augusto Ocampo in January.

1993   On February 25, Willy Romelus, the respected bishop of Jeremie, was brutally beaten by the military after conducting a mass for the nearly 1,500 victims of a ferry disaster a few days earlier.

1993   In March, the joint UN/OAS Civilian Mission in Haiti (MICIVIH) began to deploy human rights monitors throughout the country.

1993   On June 1, the National Labor Education Committee Fund in Support of Workers' and Human Rights in Central America released a report identifying policies aimed at promoting *maquiladora* industries in Haiti as having undermined both development and democracy in Haiti.

1993   On June 8, Bazin resigned as prime minister. Two weeks later the UN imposed a comprehensive fuel and arms embargo on Haiti.

1993   On July 3, after brief negotiations at Governors Island in New York, General Cedras and President Aristide signed the Governors Island Agreement. Aristide agreed to name a new prime minister, let Cedras retire before his return on October 30, and provide an amnesty for everyone involved in the coup. In return, the Parliament would enact a reform of the army and the police under the supervision of a UN mission. The UN would also lift the embargo on Haiti prior to Aristide's return.

1993   In August, in accordance with the Governors Island agreement, the members of Parliament elected illegally in January left, and the original members were allowed to return. The Parliament ratified Robert Malval,

President Aristide's nominee, as prime minister and the UN lifted the embargo. MICIVIH recorded a rapid increase in the military's repression of human rights and prodemocracy activists, with many more disappearances and killings.

1993   In September, Cedras denounced the Malval cabinet as not representative of the Governors Island accord. The same month, military attachés assassinated Antoine Izmery, prominent pro-Aristide businessman, and a new organization of paramilitary thugs, the notorious FRAPH, made its appearance. Within weeks, FRAPH members had spread a reign of terror throughout Haiti, attempted to kill pro-Aristide Senator Wesner Emmanuel and Port-au-Prince Mayor Evans Paul, and demanded that the Malval cabinet include more members of the far right.

1993   On October 11, the first contingent of U.S. and UN trainers for the military and the army arrived at Port-au-Prince on board the *Harlan County*. FRAPH thugs demonstrated noisily at the port, and the United States ordered the ship to return.

1993   On October 14, FRAPH assassinated Guy Malary, minister for justice in the Malval cabinet. On October 15, the UN reimposed the embargo on Haiti with stricter controls than before.

1993   In November, the *New York Times* revealed many links between the CIA and top Haitian military brass right up to the coup. The same month, MICIVIH reported evidence supporting direct involvement of the authorities in the killing of Antoine Izmery.

1993   On December 15, Prime Minister Malval resigned.

1993   On December 27, FRAPH burned a thousand homes, with much loss of life, in a pro-Aristide area of Cité Soleil, Port-au-Prince's largest slum, in revenge for the death of a FRAPH member.

1994   President Aristide convened a three-day conference in

Miami (January 14–16) of many different organizations that were dealing with the Haitian situation. The conference heavily criticized the U.S. policy of returning Haitian refugees without asylum hearings.

1994   Yvon Desanges, a prodemocracy activist picked up in the U.S. and repatriated to Haiti, was murdered by soldiers on January 26.

1994   MICIVIH monitors, who had left Haiti after the *Harlan County* incident, were allowed to return in small numbers by Gen. Cedras in February.

1994   The Haitian parliament proposed a revised version of the Governors Island accord on February 15. Under this new proposal, developed by the presidents of the Haitian Senate and Chamber of Deputies with the assistance of the U.S.-based Center for Democracy, the coup leaders would retire with full amnesty, the international embargo would be relaxed, and President Aristide would appoint a new prime minister to head a coalition government. The date for Aristide's return would, however, not be set. Aristide criticized the proposal, saying that no prime minister could function in Haiti under the prevailing conditions.

1994   On February 22, UN/OAS envoy Caputo announced his support of the parliamentary plan. The Chamber of Deputies approved it on March 2.

1994   On February 26, the Catholic Commission on Justice and Peace of Haiti reported massive smuggling of gasoline from the Dominican Republic. In fact, the Dominican-Haitian border remained largely porous, with heavy commercial traffic, through the period of the embargo.

1994   On March 8, U.S. Special Envoy for Haiti Lawrence Pezzullo admitted in Congress that the so-called parliamentary plan had in fact been authored by the State Department, and that the parliamentarians who developed the plan with the Center for Democracy had been handpicked by U.S. officials.

1994	On March 23, members of MICIVIH were attacked in Haiti after they issued a report pointing out that kidnappings, political murders, and random killings by FRAPH had greatly increased in the past few months.
1994	On April 4, President Aristide, due to continued U.S. refusal to hear Haitian claims to political asylum, suspended the 1981 treaty that allowed the United States to repatriate Haitians picked up at sea.
1994	On April 22, FRAPH members massacred 27 citizens in the Raboteau neighborhood of Gonaives. Three days later, they carried out a similar massacre in the village of Bassin Caiman.
1994	On April 26, Lawrence Pezzullo resigned as the special envoy for Haiti.
1994	On May 8, the United States announced a change in its refugee policy, saying that the "boat people" would be allowed to request asylum in a third country, but that only 10 percent would be granted asylum.
1994	On May 11, the junta replaced Joseph Nerette with Emile Jonassaint as president of Haiti, indicating its unwillingness to abide by any previous agreements that recognized Aristide as president.
1994	On July 31, Resolution 940 of the UN Security Council authorized the use of "all necessary means" to restore the legitimate government of Haiti. A U.S.-led Multinational Force was authorized to accomplish this. After the withdrawal of this force, the task of maintaining a secure environment would be taken over by the UN Mission in Haiti (UNMIH)—a full-fledged peacekeeping operation, not just a training mission.
1994	From September 17 to 19, a team consisting of Gen. Colin Powell, Sen. Sam Nunn, and former president Jimmy Carter persuaded the junta to leave Haiti voluntarily and let the Multinational Force land unopposed.

1994   On October 15, President Aristide was restored as the
            head of state after the junta left Haiti following the
            arrival of 21,000 U.S. troops.

NOTES

1. See Trouillot, *Haiti: State Against Nation,* pp. 35–50.
2. Ibid., pp. 59–60.
3. Ibid., p. 61.
4. Ibid., p. 89.
5. Ibid., p. 63.
6. Ibid., p. 69.
7. Ibid., pp. 97–100.
8. Ibid., p. 131.
9. Ibid., pp. 139–140.
10. Ibid., p. 148.
11. Ibid., p. 158.
12. Chapter 4 of Trouillot's *Haiti* broadly makes this point.
13. Ibid., pp. 222–223.
14. See "Words of Deliverance: 1," in Wilentz, *The Rainy Season.*

1

INTRODUCTION

WHAT IS PEACEBUILDING?

In a recent report to the United Nations Security Council, *The Causes of Conflict and the Promotion of Durable Peace and Sustainable Development in Africa,* Secretary-General Kofi Annan presented his definition of "postconflict peacebuilding."

> By postconflict peacebuilding I mean actions undertaken at the end of a conflict to consolidate peace and prevent a recurrence of armed confrontation. Experience has shown that the consolidation of peace in the aftermath of conflict requires more than a purely diplomatic and military action, and that an integrated peace-building effort is needed to address the various factors that have caused or are threatening a conflict. Peacebuilding may involve the creation or strengthening of national institutions, monitoring elections, promoting human rights, providing for reintegration and rehabilitation programs, and creating conditions for resumed development.[1]

The following six arguments can be derived from this definition:

First, the goal of postconflict peacebuilding is to prevent the recurrence of armed confrontation.

Second, to the extent that peacebuilding attempts to achieve this goal through addressing "the various factors that have caused or are threatening conflict," it can do so not only after a conflict, but also prior to the conflict. Presumably, if an all-out civil war has not occurred, one would look for other signs, including rising levels of violence and insecurity, that a wider conflict is likely.

Third, peacebuilding has no clear *modus operandi.* Depending on the target country, one or more of the activities identified in the Secretary-General's definition might be needed to prevent future conflict. While some of these activities, such as demobilization of combatants or reintegration, will only be required in postconflict situations, others such as "strengthening of national institutions" or "resumed development" are generic to most developing nations.

Fourth, different factors might be the immediate cause of conflict in the affected societies. In some societies, these factors might involve rampaging armies that need to be demobilized; in others, they might include gross human rights violations; in still others, severe underdevelopment might be a cause for conflict. In the last case particularly, peacebuilding, whether pre-conflict or postconflict, might not look very different from economic or political development. In fact, by recognizing that development might be a part of postconflict peacebuilding, the Secretary-General also implicitly recognizes that lack of development could be a cause of conflict.

Fifth, several causal factors might have operated together in bringing about conflict. In fact, the complexity of human systems almost certainly rules out single-factor causation. For instance, while a tendency to violence or a certain level of ethnic tension might exist in a society, it is unlikely that these factors will lead to all-out war in the absence of other precipitating factors such as gross poverty or ecological disaster. Similarly, poverty on its own is rarely a cause for conflict without the precipitating presence of leaders who are willing to deflect the resulting popular frustration onto any ethnic or other divisions that might exist within a society.

Finally, to the extent that a set of factors might lead to violent conflict within a society, it is reasonable to assume that a coherent global strategy for successfully managing and containing these factors would be the primary immediate factor preventing conflict. The sustainable management of violent conflict within a society would, therefore, involve a self-perpetuating mechanism that constantly creates such global strategies as the situation demands. This mechanism would have to take the form of a dynamic and adaptive process. It is important to remember that conflict is almost a continuous fact of life in most societies. The trick is to manage it so that it does not become violent. Obviously, this management would have to include more than a laundry list of international or domestic projects involving infrastructure repair, removing land mines, or expanding education. The precise components of the management process would vary from one country to another. In some they might involve formal democratic institutions; in others, an informal set of associations; in still others, the mobilization of hitherto passive sections of society.

Seen from the perspective of these arguments, peacebuilding could be defined as *the creation within a country of a self-perpetuating mechanism or process for the sustainable management of disputes in order to pre-empt violent conflict.*

Under this definition, the key question to ask of a society in the aftermath or on the verge of conflict is not "what basket of activities can be undertaken to build peace," but "what self-sustaining *process* can be initiated for the pre-emptive management of disputes." The key parameters of this process, and of the optimal international role in establishing it, should ideally be defined on the basis of consensus at the hands of a truly representative group from within the target country, with the international community playing a vital facilitatory role. While this ideal cannot be realized in all situations, a focus on process—on interlinkages and relationships—by all international and domestic parties concerned is much more likely to create a sustainable conflict management capacity within the affected society than otherwise. From this perspective, while short-term reconstruction activities such as rehabilitating basic infrastructure and providing basic amenities will undoubtedly need international support, they do not necessarily lead to a lasting peace.

In this paper, I will apply this revised understanding of peacebuilding to Haiti, and suggest that internal disputes will not be sustainably and pre-emptively managed in Haiti until a vital and substantive dialogue—aimed at developing a common vision of the country's future and a living social pact—is established between all sectors and political tendencies in the country. International attempts to assist Haiti—to build lasting peace—will only be successful in the context of the establishment of this pact. While much of what the international community is currently doing in Haiti—from building institutions to economic reform—overlaps considerably with conventional economic and political development activities, peacebuilding in Haiti will only be successful if it is recognized as such by the affected parties.

WHY PEACEBUILDING IN HAITI?

Not one of the numerous Haitian leaders with whom I have spoken in the past two years has described their country's problems in terms of "postconflict peacebuilding." Most have used the fairly standard referents for developing countries in trouble: massive unemployment, lack of efficient public institutions, environmental degradation, and so on. Coups and violence, if they happen, are attributed to these problems. These Haitian leaders do not speak of failed states, civil war, or partition, nor of long-term or short-term causes of conflict. But they do speak of sustainable political and economic development if Haiti is to avoid violence in the future.[2] And they do not, yet, talk of civil war as a means for resolving their differences over attaining such development.

Why, then, is the international community conducting "postconflict peacebuilding" in Haiti? The answer lies in the chronology of recent international involvement in the country. In the recent past, negotiated attempts to persuade an illegal coup government to give up power were termed as "peacemaking," which normally involves mediating an end to wars. A U.S.-led intervention to oust the military junta was termed as "peace enforcement," which usually implies the use of coercion by third parties to bring one or more warring parties to the negotiating table and to keep them there. Finally, a policing operation, including both training and patrolling functions, was termed "peacekeeping," which was traditionally the use of lightly armed troops to monitor ceasefires. In the standard chronology of international interventions, peacekeeping is usually accompanied and followed by postconflict peacebuilding, or assistance provided to rebuild some of the infrastructure destroyed by conflict. In Haiti, in the absence of having to rebuild after a civil war, a basket of nonmilitary activities designed to address some of the primary causes of violence—weak institutions, underdevelopment, poverty—came to be referred to as "postconflict peacebuilding."

These very same problems were also the target of the numerous development schemes that were launched throughout the developing world between 1965 and 1985, including Haiti. Of course, development is typically an open-ended process, whereas peacebuilding comes with a time limit. Enough has to be done in the context of building viable political institutions and a functioning economy within two to five years to justify the disengagement of international military forces that might have been providing stability in the absence of an effective polity or economy. Seen from the vantage point of Haiti, then, peacebuilding becomes a speeded-up version of a conventional development process.

The international community, of course, is not the only one trying to build a lasting polity and economy in Haiti. Since the departure of the Duvalier dictatorship in 1986, Haitians have struggled among themselves to define the nature, the structure, and the power base of a Haitian state that can best provide for its constituents. Into this struggle the international community has brought its own understanding of a functioning Haitian state—an understanding transplanted from states seen as being effective in the developed or newly industrialized countries—as one that is constituted through direct elections and favors a free-market economy. Many Haitians, however, disagree. Since the international community has vigorously pushed this understanding of the state against contending understandings, it has become a participant in the struggle to define the Haitian state.

From this perspective, peacebuilding is a struggle to make Haitians understand the value of a state that satisfies certain international criteria. Arguably, there are many citizens who would support a truly democratic state and a truly open economy. Yet they have never had an opportunity to participate in a real debate, or develop a consensus, over what their government should look like or be about. Peacebuilding would only be successful if Haitians themselves understand and support any given understanding of what a successful polity and economy should look like, and if they participate in bringing it about. In order to assist them in this task, or to carry out successful postconflict peacebuilding, we need to have a better understanding of the context in which we are trying to prevent further violent conflict.

In the remainder of this chapter, I first identify some of the key elements of Haiti's development dilemma and then enumerate some reasons that Haiti continues to be of significance for the international community of nations, outside of the U.S. interest in ensuring that Haitian refugees fleeing to Florida do not become an electoral issue in the United States itself. In the second chapter, I briefly outline some of the activities of the United Nations in Haiti following the restoration of the legitimate government of President Aristide in 1994, and draw some conclusions for future operations. The third chapter offers an analytical perspective on those aspects of Haitian history that are relevant in today's context. The fourth chapter explores some of the recent causes of Haiti's underdevelopment. And Chapter 5 draws upon the preceding four chapters to offer specific recommendations for peacebuilding in Haiti and, more generally, for future international activity in societies torn by internal violence or conflict.[3]

THE HAITIAN CHALLENGE

At first sight, Haiti presents a unique developmental challenge. There is no other country in the world that has suffered for so long, and so persistently, from a downward spiral of decline. Initially, following its independence, Haiti was caught in an economic stasis for nearly a century and a half. With no growth in the national product, the availability of scarce internal resources for agriculture, the country's economic mainstay, declined. In the second half of the twentieth century, development policies designed to address this crisis increased internal migration and further heightened internal tensions.

In 1994, an international military force intervened, for the second time in the country's history and in this century, to liberate Haiti from a seemingly endless cycle of coups, violence, and brutality. The jury is still out on whether Haiti's neighbors have succeeded in liberating Haitians from their own history. One thing is for certain: As Haiti undergoes momentous change in its attempts to modernize, it becomes increasingly clear that in some critical aspects, Haitians are like people anywhere else in the world.

Whether in the slums of Cité Soleil, or in the increasingly infertile farmland in the Northwest, poor Haitians display great ingenuity in developing survival strategies that often have more in common with ingenious barrio dwellers elsewhere in Latin America than with their own often fractious and unproductive ruling elite. Unlike their rulers, who only cooperate as a last resort, Haitian peasants share labor and other resources in times of adversity through peasant cooperatives. In doing so, they have more in common with the successful members of the Grameen Bank in Bangladesh than with their country's parasitical oligarchy. Like peasants elsewhere in the developing world, they find their extremely sophisticated knowledge base of local conditions being considered irrelevant by their own rulers as well as development experts. Also, like peasants elsewhere in the world, they have been derided as illiterate and therefore irrelevant by educated folks from the cities. Yet, perhaps no other ruling elite in the world has harbored such visceral disdain—perhaps even fear—of their country's peasantry than that of Haiti. Most Haitian policymakers routinely dismiss the ability of the masses to provide any substantial input into the formulation of development policy. And therein lies Haiti's tragedy. Since Haiti's violent birth, its ruling elite has maintained the gap between itself and the masses with a level of stringency and a degree of ostracization that is perhaps only matched by that of the worst years of apartheid-era South Africa.

In this paper, I will argue that because of this vast chasm, Haitians have never had the opportunity to develop a common conception of what their country is about. Haitians from all walks of life have never sat down to have a genuine national discussion about the meaning of being Haitian, about what kind of historical trajectory their nation ought to follow, and about common means for achieving national objectives. In the absence of this genuine national consensus, Haiti has lurched from one crisis to another, one deadlock to the next, for most of its history. With international forces having dismantled the predatory Haitian army after 1994, Haiti's politicians have taken their perpetual deadlock to the floor of the parliament, where the search for compromise can be as frustrating as attempts to seek good advice from the *loas,* or spirits, of the *voudoun* pantheon.

While the economics and politics of mass deprivation in Haiti might share common elements with those of other developing countries, the uniqueness of Haitian culture is undeniable. The first-time visitor to Haiti is always impressed by the remarkable vibrancy of Haitian life, with its sometimes excessive profusion of music, art, and dance. The country's dire straits do not seem to affect people in their daily lives, who go about their business of survival not with the archetypical apathy of the destitute, but with all the gusto of Wall Street brokers. Perhaps the most intriguing quality in people's lives is the obvious absence of absolutes. People, both the rich and the deprived, often give far more credence to oblique references, nebulous symbols, and outright rumor than they do to straight fact. The perception of power is often more credible than absolute knowledge of the sources of that power. Haiti's is a culture where plain statement is considered banal, and circumlocution, the use of axiomatic and metaphorical phrases, and argument for the sake of argument are hallmarks of erudition. Perhaps this cultural ambience reflects the precepts of *voudoun,* where the boundaries between the material and the spiritual, dream and reality, the mutterings of the spirit world and the three-dimensional input of our senses are thinly drawn.

Perceptual ambiguity plagues not only everyday lives, but also the realm of politics. While the elite in Haiti may be separated from the masses by a gulf greater than that of any other developing country, the boundaries of this gulf are not as stark as those in say, Guatemala, or in South Africa, in the recent past. In fact, in these and other countries that have faced revolutionary struggles against heinous repression, the lines between the forces of regression and progression, of dark and light, have been quite starkly drawn. This has helped speed along a process of national renewal, since obstacles to progress could be clearly identified and targeted. This is not the situation in Haiti, where the ruling elite have always presented themselves as inheritors of history's only successful slave revolt. While they have always emphasized French education, language, and religion, the elites have also always understood Creole and turned to the *houngans*—the *voudoun* priests—as a last resort in times of trouble, thereby making Haiti one of the most culturally cohesive of the developing states. Mindful of the blood shed by the common slaves—who subsequently became independent peasants—in ridding Haiti of the French, the elite have never directly oppressed the peasants. Instead, an insidious system of exploitation, under which mercantile middle-men appropriate most of the peasant surplus, has been used to keep the peasants in penury. Furthermore, the elite have traditionally been adept at wrapping themselves in the trappings of legitimate political discourse, which has often hidden agendas for personal gain. For instance, the debate over the role of populism, as opposed to techno-cratic ability, in forming government policy had usually appeared in Haiti history either right after, or prior to, the formation of dictatorial regimes.[4] As in Haiti today, it has not led to any substantive outcomes.

Without any clear, overwhelming rationale on the side of either the elite or the peasantry for an intensive, revolutionary encounter, Haiti has until very recently lacked the dialectic to launch itself out of its entropic stupor. International development schemes in the 1970s and 1980s pushed many peasants into the cities to provide cheap labor for new assembly industries. Here, face to face with their rulers, the peasants acquired new insights into the former's parasitic tenden-cies. This knowledge traveled throughout Haiti on the back of the Haitian incarnation of the liberation theology movement within the Catholic Church. The *ti Legliz* (the Little Church) proved instrumen-tal in mobilizing a countrywide array of peasant and worker organiza-tions that were formed for the sole purpose of giving the hitherto dis-empowered *mounn andeyo* (the "people outside") a voice in their country's government. The struggle to establish this voice, and to cre-ate a system of governance that recognized and met its demands, led to the cycle of events that prompted the international intervention of 1994. For the first time since Haiti's struggle for independence, the lines between progression and regression were again clear. Perhaps no other government in Haiti's history has been so devoid of external and internal legitimacy as the military dictatorship that overthrew elected President Aristide in 1991. Yet while Haitians from all sectors and from the diaspora in North America came together to overthrow this government, they have yet to create a similar joint effort to build their country in the aftermath of its departure. In the meantime, much of the energy and many of the ideas generated in the groundswell of popular mobilization since the mid-1980s have begun to dissipate. It is as if having found the magic words to open the Aladdin's cave of opportunity, Haiti is hesitant to enter through the portals. The question, of course, is whether the door will shut again before Haitians can make a move.

When viewed from an airplane during a flight into the country, the Haitian landscape resembles an entity that has waited so long for deliverance that it has started to crumble. The denuded hillsides and the cactus-ridden sand flats—all a contradiction in a lush Caribbean climate—are a stark reminder of lost possibilities. The mouths of river estuaries can be clearly seen vomiting the country's topsoil into its bays. One is reminded of an old woman bleeding to death from all pores. As the plane comes in low, the smoke from an occasional wood fire can be seen rising into the sky, destroying whatever little is left of the country's forest cover and its future. The overwhelming sense of gloom and lassitude engendered by this vista lasts only as long as it takes to disembark from the plane and meet the cheerfully clothed welcoming band at the entrance to Port-au-Prince's small international airport. Disembarking passengers accomplish feats of athletic prowess as they attempt to retrieve their baggage from the battered conveyor belt. Outside, chaos reigns as competing taxi drivers try to grab your luggage. Young children trail you and sing praises of your ancestors as they attempt to relieve you of your change. On the road from the airport to Port-au-Prince, the landscape is a cacophony of near-death vehicles scrambling over potholes, trucks belching diesel fuel, and the four-wheel drives of international organizations trying to carry their harried charges to an assortment of air-conditioned offices. Amidst all this flurry of so many Haitians all trying to get somewhere, lassitude and comfortable inertia beckon in the form of tropical rum, poolside soirees at elite hotels, and concert nights at the Hotel Olofsson.[5]

Haiti on the ground shares an important common characteristic with Haiti as seen from the air—whether gloomy or energetic, the Haitian vista is primarily that of entropy. Ideas and organized activity, as much as buildings and roads, have a brief day in the sun, and then crumble very rapidly into Brownian motion, a very low-level equilibrium in which higher forms of organization are practically alien. A friend once compared Haiti to a fetid Florida marsh. Like the marsh, the immediate impression one gets on looking at Haiti is of chaos. Looking through the chaos, however, one sees many different forms of organization. As with the flora and the fauna in a marsh, the denizens of Haiti seemed to be engaged in profoundly energetic though endlessly repetitive cycles of activity. While Haiti appears to be moving ahead, it never gets anywhere. In the same manner that the thick water of the marsh, if disturbed, returns quickly to its original placidity, ideas and new activity only disturb Haiti for so long before being submerged by eternity.[6] Haiti presents the same gloomy vista of stillness and timelessness that a marsh does, but with an undercurrent of life and vibrancy that is equally timeless. Of course, as with a marsh, Haiti induces a languid stupor in the frequent visitor. As with the marsh, its mysteries, its fundamental essence, have yet to be plumbed by outsiders. While you can never really understand a marsh, you can definitely drain it and change it for ever. Similarly, several scholars have recently suggested that the only way to lift Haiti out of its low-level equilibrium is through an external shock.[7] We don't as yet have enough knowledge of the country to know what the local impacts of this external shock would be.[8] But one thing is increasingly clear, and this is where the analogy with the marsh ends: Any attempts to induce fundamental change in the country without the participation of the majority of its population would destroy the country forever.

THE SIGNIFICANCE OF HAITI

Apart from the U.S. interest in keeping Haitian refugees from the shores of Florida, why should this tiny, impoverished island nation of 7 million be of interest to the world? Several reasons come to mind.

The first reason can only be stated with a certain amount of trepidation in today's politically correct world. Despite similarities between Haiti and other developing countries, Haiti's condition of exceptional stasis or entropy is often condescendingly explained in private conversations by international officials as originating from the fact that the country was founded through the world's only successful slave rebellion. While the slaves learned to overthrow their masters, they had learned little of the science of government. By contrast, Haiti's neighbors that spent more years under colonial tutelage have perfomed much better. This line of reasoning is similar to that espoused by a British prime minister in the nineteenth century who argued that, in the absence of European tutelage, the African peoples showed little genius for government. For those of us who are of a politically correct bent and who therefore disagree with such racially biased arguments, the burden of proving that the causes for Haiti's uniquely intractable poverty lie elsewhere becomes a big one, which requires us to expend a considerable amount of time in gaining a more sophisticated understanding of the country and its circumstances.

Haiti also stands at the cusp of another cultural debate. On a statistical basis, those developing nations that were British colonies have done much better on the economic and political fronts than the colonies of such Latin nations such as France, Spain, and Portugal. While former British colonies include failed states such as Sierra Leone, and Latin colonies include such stars of the developing world as Chile, Brazil, and Côte d'Ivoire, the argument has repeatedly been espoused that an Anglo-Saxon tradition of governance lends itself more easily to democratic practices than a Latin one. While this debate can hardly be resolved in Haiti, the Haitian situation presents a far more nuanced set of circumstances than the debate would suggest. While Haiti has been largely a failure on the political and economic fronts, it has developed a vibrant Afro-European culture that, despite the country's destitution, attracts connoisseurs of food, music, and art from around the world,[9] and which has also served as an inspiration to numerous other artists—including Harry Belafonte, Graham Greene, and Richard Morse of the rara band RAM to name a few. At the very least, this vibrant uniqueness reminds us not to look at countries as mere artifacts of their colonial heritage.

The third reason for Haiti's current significance is that it is the site of a unique experiment. Haiti does not represent the first time that the international community has sought fundamentally to alter a nation's political and economic parameters under the peacekeeping umbrella. Prior to the debacle in Somalia, such alterations were attempted in Cambodia[10] and El Salvador with some measure of success. Following Somalia, the same exercise was continued under different guises in Mozambique and Bosnia-Herzegovina, with an even greater input of international resources and heavier external control. In all these cases, though, international involvement took place in the context of a civil war that had destroyed most of the host country's political and economic infrastructure. However, Haiti had not seen a civil war since the aborted Christophe monarchy in the early nineteenth century. International involvement in Haiti happened solely as a result of the consequences of the country's underdevelopment being felt on the shores of its most powerful neighbor. In an era where the internal circumstances of countries are translated beyond their boundaries through flows of goods, people, ideas, and media images, this would not be the last time that a country's underdevelopment would become the subject of concerted external intervention. Rather than seeing longer term development planning as was attempted from the 1960s to the 1980s, we might see speeded-up development under the guise of peacekeeping or other forms of crisis management. Terms such as "conflict prevention" and "preventive peacebuilding," which often operationally translate into development-type activities, are already becoming a part of the international lexicon. Recently, the specter of thousands of refugees fleeing crisis-struck Indonesia prompted concerted and preventive emergency action by an number of international organizations and external governments. As one of the first cases of accelerated development under the conflict management umbrella, Haiti might provide useful pointers for the next decade.

A key question on the economic front that remains unanswered for many developing nations, and is particularly acute for those that lack a sizeable middle class, is that of reconciling the market imperatives of creating growth and generating investor confidence with the primary domestic imperative of ensuring that the basic needs of the population are met. Government spending to obtain the latter objectives usually reduces an economy's competitiveness in the world economy. An exclusive emphasis on export-oriented growth, however, might create the kinds of internal tension that have brought Haiti to its current impasse. And it is not just the economies of the affected countries that are at stake on the adequate resolution of this question. As the recent bailouts of the Mexican economy and those of several East Asian countries suggest, the futures of many fund managers on whom the middle classes of the developed world have rested their hopes for long-term prosperity are also at stake. Haiti provides us with a unique opportunity to develop some suitable answers in this regard. Its economic size is practically insignificant, and it can therefore serve as the venue for a certain amount of economic experimentation that would not immediately be thwarted by global market reaction. Also, the crisis management umbrella for international involvement in Haiti could impart a greater urgency to the search for appropriate economic answers.

2

THE UN AND HAITI TODAY

HISTORY OF UN INVOLVEMENT

The most recent phase of UN involvement in Haiti began in September 1991, when the democratically elected government of President Aristide was overthrown by a military government led by General Raoul Cedras and forced to flee. The international community responded swiftly and embarked on what turned out to be a three-year process of sanctions and negotiations with the military regime before President Aristide's eventual return to power in 1994.

The response of the Organization of American States (OAS) and the Caribbean Community (CARICOM) was especially vigorous, spurred by both the OAS's new commitment to the consolidation of representative democracy in the hemisphere, and the instrumental role played by both organizations in facilitating and monitoring the election that had won Aristide the presidency.[11] The OAS rapidly suspended all aid to Haiti except humanitarian assistance. When, several days later, the OAS delegation negotiating with the military regime was ordered to leave the country, the organization called on members to impose a trade embargo. Meanwhile, a violent crackdown on political opponents by the military regime began a Haitian exodus to the United States.

In the fall of 1992, Secretary-General Boutros-Ghali authorized a joint OAS/UN mission to Haiti to negotiate with the government, and a special envoy for Haiti, Dante Caputo, was soon appointed (shortly thereafter, he was also named OAS special envoy). General Cedras and the Haitian prime minister, Marc Bazin, indicated that they wanted to cooperate. Writing to Caputo in January 1993, they accepted a proposal to establish a joint OAS/UN civilian mission to monitor human rights. Under the terms of the agreement, the mission would have full freedom of movement, monitor human rights in accordance with the Haitian constitution and relevant international conventions, and make recommendations to Haitian authorities as well as verify their implementation. The Cedras regime also agreed to work toward rebuilding Haiti's frail institutions under the leadership of the special envoy. On April 10, 1993, the joint human rights mission, the International Civilian Mission to Haiti (MICIVIH), was authorized by the UN General Assembly[12]; and it had submitted its first report by early June.

Caputo's efforts to engage the Haitian military in dialogue were not successful, however; on June 16, 1993, the Security Council placed an oil and arms embargo upon Haiti, acting under Chapter VII of the UN Charter.[13]

Immediately following the imposition of the embargo, Cedras again indicated a willingness to negotiate and began the talks that resulted in the Governors Island Agreement, signed on July 3, 1993 (named for the location of the talks in New York). The Governors Island Agreement pledged Cedras to retire from government and allow Aristide's return to Haiti by October 30. In the interim, Aristide would work with the Haitian parliament to restore normal functioning among Haiti's institutions, and the United Nations would provide a small force to help modernize the armed forces and create a new civilian police force.

Initial signs were promising, with the Haitian parliament ratifying Aristide's appointment for prime minister (Robert Malval), on August 25, and the Security Council lifting the embargo on Haiti and authorizing a United Nations Mission in Haiti (UNMIH).[14]

The promise turned sour quickly, however, when the UNMIH advance team arrived in the Port-au-Prince harbor on October 11, was met by hostile demonstrations, and turned back, prompting the flight of most of MICIVIH's personnel. The Security Council rapidly reimposed the arms and oil embargo. The Haitian junta followed this action by assassinating Aristide's justice minister, François-Guy Malary, on October 15. By early 1994, the few remaining MICIVIH personnel reported an alarming increase in human rights violations. Facing continued intransigence from the military government, the Security Council imposed a comprehensive set of sanctions on Haiti, to which the regime responded by appointing a "provisional" president (Emile Jonassaint) who formally expelled MICIVIH from the country on July 11, 1994.

By 1994, the deteriorating situation in Haiti had loosed a surge of refugees on American shores, thus putting domestic pressure on the Clinton administration, especially from Florida, which bore the brunt of the refugee wave. Additional pressure for U.S. action came from the Congressional Black Caucus and influential African-American organizations such as TransAfrica. The upshot was the adoption on July 30, 1994, of Security Council Resolution 940, which authorized the formation of a multinational force under Chapter VII of the UN Charter:

> to use all necessary means to facilitate the departure from Haiti of the military leadership, consistent with the Governors Island agreement, the prompt return of the legitimately elected President and the restoration of the legitimate authorities of the Government of Haiti, and to establish and maintain a secure and stable environment that will permit implementation of the Governors Island agreement....

The U.S.-led Multinational Force, or MNF, would then be replaced by an expanded UNMIH, which would be responsible for sustaining the secure and stable environment established during the multinational phase and protecting international personnel and key installations, and for the professionalization of the Haitian armed forces and the creation of a separate police force.

Even with the passage of Res. 940 and preparations for MNF deployment, it wasn't until mid-September that President Clinton declared all diplomatic measures exhausted. Faced with impending invasion, the Cedras regime appealed for an eleventh-hour intercession. After skillful negotiation by former President Jimmy Carter, General Colin Powell, and U.S. Senator Sam Nunn, Haiti's military leaders agreed to resign with an amnesty from the Haitian parliament. As a result, the MNF was able to move into Haiti on September 19 without opposition. Operating with flexible rules of engagement, the MNF was able to respond decisively to any resistance (which may explain why it was challenged on only one occasion) and to implement its mandate effectively, including collecting large numbers of weapons from supporters of the former regime. The MNF also created an Interim Public Security Force (IPSF) from new recruits and the remnants of the old army to provide temporary security until a completely new civilian police could be fielded. President Aristide returned to Haiti on October 15, 1994.

Shortly following the MNF's arrival came a new UNMIH advance team (under Lakhdar Brahimi) and the returning core group of MICIVIH (under Colin Granderson). By January 10, 1995, the Security Council declared that a safe and secure environment had been established and that UNMIH could assume the reins from the MNF, a pattern of following a Chapter VII operation with peacekeeping that had been tried in Iraq and would subsequently be seen in Bosnia under NATO. On March 31, 1995, command transferred from the MNF to UNMIH under U.S. Major-General Joseph Kinzer.

By the time that it concluded in February 1996, UNMIH had overseen parliamentary and presidential elections for Haiti. Although the first election was marred by irregularities, and the second by low voter turnout, both were largely free and fair and conducted without violence. The presidential election had also culminated in the first democratic transition of executive power in Haiti's history, when President Aristide passed the presidency on to President René Preval on February 7, 1996.

UNMIH had also helped the Haitian government to establish a new 5,000-strong Haitian National Police (HNP) and a Haitian National Police Training Center (HNPTC). Once the HNP was fielded, the IPSF was disbanded.

My conversations with UNMIH officials in 1996 revealed that they were acutely aware that generations of dictatorship and plunder by a small elite had left the economy in shambles and the population with no experience of or faith in legitimate, responsive governance. Massive unemployment and pervasive lack of capacity to respond to popular needs at all levels of government were, arguably, the main catalysts of violence among the destitute population. Although "peacebuilding" is not seen as a proper mission of peacekeepers, especially by those who fund peacekeeping, UNMIH tried to address some of these sources of violence by interpreting its mandate to sustain a secure and stable environment in a more comprehensive way. It worked closely with international financial institutions and was also the first UN mission to integrate the work of the United Nations Development Program (UNDP) into its overall mission, naming as second in command at UNMIH the resident representative for UNDP in Haiti.

THE CURRENT SITUATION

At the time of writing in spring 1998, Haiti's prospects did not look as bright as they had when UNMIH had left the country. In December 1997, almost three years after the U.S.-led Multinational Force had intervened to restore and stabilize democratic rule in the country, the United Nations Security Council authorized a UN civilian police mission to succeed the peacekeeping operation that had ended in November.[15] This mission, the United Nations Civilian Police Mission in Haiti (MIPONUH), had followed the UN Transition Mission in

Haiti (UNTMIH), which had been instituted in August 1997. The UNTMIH had been preceded by the UN Support Mission in Haiti (UNSMIH) which had held the fort from February 1996, after the departure of UNMIH, until July 1997.

Despite the best efforts and intentions of the peacekeepers, little had changed in Haiti as a result of the intervention, aside from Aristide's triumphal return on the back of the MNF, and the existence of a shaky, rookie police force in the place of the former Forces Armée d'Haiti (FADH). The international community had supported Aristide in abolishing the army following his restoration, and had simultaneously created a new police force, the Haitian National Police (HNP) that would provide internal security.[16] In fact, by July 1997, strengthening this police force had become the rationale for the continued UN presence.

At the time of writing, several independent assessments of the force had concluded that it was at best mildly successful in maintaining security, at worst murderous; most of the times, it was simply inept.[17] I disagree with these assessments. The remarkable skill, determination, and persistence of the UN Civilian Police (UN CIVPOL) in building Haiti's police from scratch deserved praise. The new police force was a heroic accomplishment against great odds. Working without critical resources and a middle level of leadership, the force had nonetheless built up a cadre that followed rules, remained neutral in many disputes, and often did a good job of basic law enforcement. The force's director at the time of writing, Pierre Denize, was reputed to be one of the most honest and efficient civil servants in Haiti.[18] While accidental shootings and botched operations occasionally blemished the force's record, these could be attributed to growing pains rather than to gross inefficiency or a pattern of systematic violation of human rights.

I remember first seeing the members of the new police in Petionville, a suburb of Port-au-Prince, in February 1996. They appeared apprehensive, nervous, and more prone to huddling in the middle of a thoroughfare in clumps rather than conducting active policing. By October 1997, I saw a new confidence in the police. Driving through Mirabelais, La Chapelle, and Saint Marc with a UN information-gathering team, I saw police who still lacked a lot of basic equipment, including adequate uniforms and communications, but who nonetheless clearly appeared to be patrolling and guiding traffic with much greater felicity than before. Members of international organizations working in Port-au-Prince told me that the streets were definitely safer to walk in at night than most streets in many major U.S. cities. However, as with everything else in Haiti, what was left unsaid aroused much more fear than that which was clear. It was not clear whether the several high-profile murders that had taken place in the past couple of years had been criminal acts, as claimed by the government, or acts of political violence. Certainly the HNP's nascent investigative activities had not delivered on this front. From the taxi driver who picked me up at the airport to several politicians, I heard whispered accusations that a high-stakes political game was behind these killings. While rumors persisted on all sides, hard evidence was not forthcoming. The presence of a new, highly trained, and very visible rapid reaction unit within the HNP had not helped public confidence either. Shortly before I visited Haiti in April 1998, a group of bandits had briefly taken over the rural town of Mirabelais and lynched the police chief, who was reputedly an activist against corruption. While this may have been a completely criminal act, the bandits, sensing the inflamed state of political tensions in Haiti, claimed a political rationale for their actions. Once again, given these tensions, there were certainly some who believed them.

One fact that was very obvious at the time of writing was the level of fear and suspicion among the political class, many of whom lived behind high walls, protected by private security guards. In fact, the fear among the political elite far surpassed that among the civilian population.[19] Throughout the fall and spring of 1997–1998, I heard many gloomy predictions about the state of affairs approaching an all-out civil war if the existing political impasse continued. While these predictions were undoubtedly overstated, given Haitian history and the current state of affairs, several international observers told me that they had heard of a number of political figures amassing private security guards in anticipation of wider conflict.[20]

More worrisome than the abilities of the police was the fact that three years of international focus on security in Haiti had not produced even the beginnings of a functioning judiciary. Without this judiciary, and without any roots in the surrounding society, the HNP could never function effectively, no matter how well-trained or competent.[21]

At the time of writing, Haiti's democratic government was also caught in a major political impasse.[22] In order to establish the principle of peaceful transference of power via elections, and in accordance with the Haitian constitution (which bars two consecutive terms for an individual), the international community had pressured President Aristide not to run for a second term, even though some argued that he was exceptionally entitled to run a second time since he had been unable to serve most of his first term. Many Haitians apparently supported this second argument. Only 35 percent of the electorate showed up to vote in the largely free and fair presidential elections in 1995, in which Preval was elected successor to Aristide. Subsequent electoral participation also declined. The most recent legislative and municipal elections on April 6, 1997, saw a meager 5 percent voter turnout.

The international community had also pressured both Aristide and Preval to implement a tough program of economic reform and made all assistance to Haiti conditional on the implementation of this reform. While the first aspect of this reform program, the partial privatization of nine state-owned enterprises, stumbled along on the back of a broad consensus,[23] other aspects such as the trimming of the state bureaucracy and government expenditure had stalled because of opposition from Aristide, who remained Haiti's most popular political figure even after Preval succeeded him as president. Aristide argued that these reforms would benefit a small elite and cause great suffering to the majority of the population. At the time of writing, his opposition had brought the governmental process in Haiti to a complete standstill.

Complicating this standoff was a dispute over the elections of April 6, 1997, in which supporters of Aristide's Famille Lavalas group[24] had emerged ahead of their opponents; the opponents subsequently claimed that Haiti's Electoral Council, allegedly dominated by Aristide sympathizers, had permitted electoral malpractices that had facilitated Aristide's lead. The international community had also lent their support to the opposition's claims of fraud.[25] At the time of writing, this contentious issue remained unresolved. Furthermore, it led to the resignation of Prime Minister Rony Smarth in June 1997, further paralyzing the government.

Several economic trends also pointed to a bleak future, including the continuing decline of Haitian agriculture. Haiti, which was self-sufficient in food till the 1970s, was spending nearly 15 percent of its budget on imported food by 1997. Instead of creating dynamic agribusinesses, as had been anticipated by those external donors that had launched the structural transformation of Haitian agriculture in the 1970s and 1980s, international aid had largely resulted in the further decline of the Haitian peasantry. This in turn had accelerated flight from the villages to the already overburdened cities.[26] In the industrial sector, little foreign investment had come into Haiti. Expatriate Haitians, who had fled the country on grounds of insecurity, had not taken advantage of the UN presence to reenter their country. The assembly sector, long touted as the primary growth engine for Haiti, largely remained in the shambles it had been reduced to following the embargo against the military regime. The few industries that continued to function offered no backward or forward linkages into the Haitian economy.

It should be emphasized that UN peacekeeping in Haiti, under UNMIH as well as in the post-UNMIH phase, had been extremely efficient, well coordinated, and without any casualties. The security environment in Haiti had improved so drastically since the restoration of the legitimate government in October 1994 that the various UN peacekeeping operations—UNMIH, UNSMIH, UNTMIH—could all legitimately claim to have largely fulfilled their mandate. This outcome could be attributed in part to excellent leadership, and in part to the fact that, in the absence of war, there was no peace to keep in Haiti. In fact, the primary armed activity of international forces in Haiti had been to perform basic police functions.[27] Without detracting from the abilities of UN peacekeepers, I will argue that the most recent international efforts to develop Haiti have so far not borne fruit because inadequate attention has been given to the highly peculiar combination of internal and external factors in Haiti's past that have led to the failure of the Haitian state.

A word must also be said here about MICIVIH, which continued operating in Haiti at the time of writing under Colin Granderson's leadership. During the years of the coup government, MICIVIH monitors had done a heroic job of following and recording the horrible human rights violations of the illegal government even as they faced great harassment and intimidation. In 1996, many observers in Haiti had told me that MICIVIH monitors could go into some of the worst areas of Cité Soleil and still be welcomed with warmth and friendship. During the darkest hours of the dictatorship, they were the only chance that the poor had to be able to speak out against the injustices committed against them. Following the restoration of democracy, MICIVIH has done an excellent job in assisting with building greater sensitivity among the various institutions of the Haitian government on human rights issues, and in assisting with further developing the efficiency and training of the police and the judiciary. It has also assisted the organizations of civil society in developing initiatives for increased popular participation in the electoral process, and in the broader process of government.

UN PEACEKEEPING "LESSONS"

Observers of UN peacekeeping have always sifted through specific UN operations to derive lessons for future ones. UN peacekeeping in Haiti, while different from all other UN operations because there was no peace to keep in the military sense, also lends itself to such analysis. The following can be offered as "lessons" from the Haitian experience:

Where an international peacekeeping operation is being used as an umbrella for a broad-based restructuring of a country's economic and political parameters, it becomes extremely critical to ensure that the different facets of this restructuring are congruent and well coordinated with each other in order to avoid pulling different sectors of society in different and perhaps contradictory directions. In Haiti, the UN has tried to coordinate most activities through the office of the Special Representative of the Secretary-General (SRSG), who is the civilian head of the peacekeeping mission. For instance, the representative of the United Nations Development Program (UNDP) in Haiti, the UN's chief officer for economic development in the country, is also the deputy SRSG. While this has generally ensured that the UN speaks with one voice in Haiti, that is not necessarily true of all international actors. For instance, following the disputed elections of April 6, 1997, while the United States initially considered the elections fair,[28] the UN perceived them as flawed and subsequently withdrew electoral assistance. While one can only speculate, a more coordinated response from the international community might have helped to prevent the subsequent domestic impasse over the electoral issue.

Many students of UN peacekeeping have pointed towards the difference that the personal qualities of the SRSG can make in ensuring positive results. The roles played by Blondin Beye and Aldo Ajello in Angola and Mozambique respectively are pointed out in this regard. Westendorp's successfully activist role as the high representative of the international community in Bosnia-Herzegovina is often compared with the more staid style of his predecessor. As late as April 1998, more than two years after Lakhdar Brahimi's departure from Haiti, several leading political figures of different ideological persuasions fondly remembered Brahimi's tenure as the SRSG during the MNF and the UNMIH phases of the international peacekeeping in Haiti. "He was a true friend of Haiti," one commentator remarked to me. The high praise heaped on Brahimi was not so much a comment on his successors—Enrique ter Horst and the incumbent, Julian Harston, who are both diplomats of considerable standing and experience who performed well under trying circumstances—as much as a recognition of his own unique ability to take the lead in forging compromise. This ability is also reflected in his recent successes in Iraq and Afghanistan.

Another important lesson has been learned in Haiti regarding different "peacekeeping" styles. In a context such as Haiti, where international troops are essentially performing a policing function, a peacekeeping style characterized by a heavy dose of community relations becomes almost compulsory. This kind of peacekeeping is definitely more proactive than that required in an operation that serves as a tripwire or a monitor along a cease-fire line. However, it does not require the force posture of a peace enforcement operation. To the extent that the peacekeepers' security can be threatened by general lawlessness and expressions of public grievance over shortages of basic goods and amenities, effective intelligence-gathering on these matters as well as a conscious building of good relations with community leaders become essential for the tactical success of the operation. In Haiti, Pakistani peacekeepers, who were well attuned to the limitations and possibilities of patrolling in a developing country, took concrete steps to establish good relations with local officials as well as community leaders and to identify the grievances of the population in their zones of operation. Where possible, they assisted communities with small low-technology projects that addressed local needs, which could be sustained using local resources once the peacekeepers left. The goodwill these activities had generated among the local population was evident to me during a visit to Cap Haitien in February 1996. A similar approach was adopted by U.S. civil affairs teams, who were mostly drawn from the reserves and therefore better attuned to community activities than Army regulars or the Marines. It is important to note that none of these activities were specifically decreed under the mandates of any of the various peacekeeping operations approved in Haiti by the Security Council. However, commanders on the ground creatively interpreted their general mandate to ensure local security and the security of their troops as including better community relations. A lot of much-needed, sustainable local infrastructure was being built as a result.

3

HAITI SINCE INDEPENDENCE

THE WAR OF INDEPENDENCE

Due to a lack of understanding of Haiti's past, some aspects of current international policy have been significantly off the mark. The development policies backed by the international community in the 1970s and the 1980s are also partly responsible for Haiti's current plight. Unfortunately, the premises behind these policies also underlie many of the recommendations being made today. If we are to assist in building a Haiti where violence and terror are a thing of the past, it is crucial to avoid repeating past mistakes.

Perhaps the single most important element to understand about contemporary Haiti is that it remains the only nation in history to have been founded by slaves who overthrew their masters. As Sidney W. Mintz so appropriately puts it, "What Spartacus was crucified for failing to do, the Haitian people did."[29] This unique aspect of Haitian history is both an asset and a liability. While pride in their historic accomplishment allows Haitians to think of themselves as one nation despite the yawning social gulf that divides the top from the bottom, this same pride also creates an inward focus that prevents many Haitians from learning from others. Most international officials who have dealt with Haiti will surely recall the frustrating moment where, when they began to suggest remedies for Haiti's problems on the basis of the experience of other developing countries, they were reminded that their recommendations were intellectually stimulating but did not apply because Haiti was different.

Colonial Haiti was the gem of the Caribbean. With freewheeling ports and large plantations that grew tobacco, coffee, and molasses for Europe, Haiti had the biggest economy in the region.[30] A critical feature of this economy were the *gens de couleur,* or people of mixed race, the offspring of French plantation owners and slave women. The plantation owners usually educated their progeny and often signed over land titles to them. According to Mintz, a third of the land in Haiti was owned by *gens de couleur* at the beginning of Haiti's war of independence.[31]

Trouillot points to yet another critical feature of this slave economy under colonialism. The French not only sired children with their slaves but also let most slaves farm small vegetable plots on their estates. For slaves who were otherwise horribly repressed, these plots became their central focus, the only positive elements in their lives. When all else was done, the slave could return to his plot, where he was free to cultivate as he wished. For many slaves, the epitome of all evil thus became the organized labor force, where they took orders from overseers, and the pinnacle of achievement became the ownership of one's own plot of land. When the slaves drove the French away, they chose not to continue the plantation economy with its organized labor force that had made Haiti so prosperous, but instead divided the land into an egalitarian system of small landholdings geared towards subsistence agriculture, which produced only modest surpluses. In this, they predated rural Maoism by a century and a half.

Smallholding might have been a peasant virtue, but it certainly did not appeal to the *gens de couleur*. While the prolonged war of independence wiped out the French plantation-owning class, enough *gens de couleur* supported the revolutionaries to survive and become key players in post-independence Haiti. They reshaped themselves into a mercantile class that, by forming alliances with a largely black military elite, quickly took control of what soon became an extractive state.[32] Color, however, was not the primary factor in the class division that emerged.[33] The primary division was between a mercantile elite who derived their income from taxing the export of the peasant surplus, and a peasantry whose modest surpluses were expropriated for consumption by the urban elite. This primarily economic division was reinforced by a cultural division in which the urban elite spoke French, equated erudition with a French education, and practiced Catholicism. The peasantry, on the other hand, spoke Creole, placed a premium on practical knowledge of agriculture, and sought spiritual succor from the deities of *voudoun*.

It is important to remember that the urban elites did not force the peasants to pay taxes. That would have been tantamount to reestablishing slavery, an institution against which both the peasants and the elites had fought together. The peasants were allowed the right to farm their own plots of land, a right they had won from the plantation owners and one that defined Haitian nationhood.[34]

However, increasingly high taxes were levied by the Haitian state via customs houses on the export of the peasant produce. The middlemen who brought this produce to the ports passed these taxes on to the peasants. Eventually, customs house receipts became the mainstay of the Haitian state. The state came to be organized not to reinvest in factors of production in agriculture, or to grow the economy, but to merely collect revenues.[35] Haitian politics became centered around struggles among various urban groups to obtain the greatest chunk of these revenues. Politicians became more obsessed with the procedure and ritual of politics, which affected their ability to grab the state's bounty for their constituencies, than with larger social and economic issues. To this day, Haitian politics remains centered around which leader can obtain the biggest state bounty for his or her constituency and still lacks a longer-term discourse.[36]

Another important aspect of Haiti's struggle for independence was the prolonged brutality of the fighting.[37] Plantation owners and slaves matched each other killing for gratuitous killing. Tens of thousands were butchered on all sides. Images of both plantation owners and their slaves being gutted and lynched alongside their families in esoterically cruel ways still appear in Haitian art and imagination. For those among Haiti's elite who survived the carnage, the memories of hitherto meek but suddenly bloodthirsty slaves stalking the countryside were indelibly printed on the collective memory. Adding to the trauma was the explanation given for the slaves' prowess and confidence. Illiterate slaves beat back the armies of France, one of the world's greatest powers, because of the magic of *voudoun,* as exemplified in the magical persona of their leader Toussaint de l'Ouverture. The slaves were the not the only ones who believed this. Many elite survivors were at a loss otherwise to explain how, despite the glories of their civilization, the French lost. While an obvious secular explanation would have looked towards the natural advantages enjoyed by a guerilla army operating on familiar terrain against a more centralized foreign force, Haiti's miasmic ambience undoubtedly lent greater credence to *voudoun*-based explanations. It is likely that these attitudes prompted a historical fear of the peasantry on the part of the elite.

Because of these schisms, the defining characteristic of the Haitian economy for the past two centuries has been the absence of any capital accumulation by the state or the private sector in the rural or urban areas. Trouillot points out that the sixty-year embargo slapped on Haiti by foreign powers in the nineteenth century for daring to overthrow its colonial masters stunted the development of the Haitian economy by making it more profitable for Haitian and foreign merchants to exploit loopholes in the embargo than make investments in fixed capital.[38] Additionally, since they did not control the rural peasantry, who resisted being herded back into plantations, the urban elite did not make long-term investments in agriculture, and contented themselves with taxing the peasant. Haiti's economy thus achieved a state of stasis, and has remained there since.[39]

From the perspective of building a stable Haiti today, therefore, it is important to grasp that the extractive nature of the state that emerged from the war of independence has been the biggest deterrent to development. This extractive state has lasted into the present. As long as the contemporary state is not organized to provide leadership for all Haitians in creating a stable framework for growth, it does not matter whether a few enterprises are owned by the public or the private sector, or whether elections are held with greater or lesser frequency, or held at all. Even elected officials will go back to bickering over the spoils of the state, as they have been doing since the restoration of democracy in 1994. In fact, what may appear to foreign officials as substantive debates over economic reform or electoral policy largely hide intensely competitive personal agendas within small elite groups. A modern Haitian activist who has consistently attempted to raise herself above this bickering once told me that while she fully supported the efficient delivery of services to consumers, looking for options to obtain this delivery in terms of state versus private ownership made little sense in Haiti. Both state and private enterprises would usually be owned by the same extended network of individuals with close ties. Privatization would simply lead to the transfer of enterprises from one set of corrupt hands to another. Haiti had not yet attained the level of industrial sophistication to have clearly differentiated public and private sectors.

Despite all of these drawbacks, Haiti's war of independence also produced one of the country's greatest assets which, even today, could form the basis for a national renaissance. According to Ernst Preeg, former U.S. ambassador to Haiti:

> Finally, and pervading all other aspects of Haitian national character, is a profound and composite feeling of national identity, pride, and self-confidence. National identity stems from the internalized historical experience of an island nation—half an island actually— thousands of miles from its African roots and constantly isolated from or threatened by closer neighbors. Haitians are forceful in asserting their distinctive identity.... In Haiti, *blanc* (white) applies to all foreigners no matter what their skin pigment. The feeling of national pride derives from the historical experience of having struggled and triumphed over natural adversity and so many exter-

nal threats.... Individual self-confidence is the most remarkable
Haitian trait.... Haitian workers at home rise quickly to any opportunity, confident of doing a good job.[40]

While historical circumstances have kept Haitian entrepreneurship at
bay within Haiti itself, these traits make Haitians formidable entrepreneurs in New York, Miami, and Montreal. One of the development
challenges before contemporary Haiti is to harness this entrepreneurship for Haiti itself.

When looking at Haiti from the outside, most foreign analysts
equate entrepreneurship either with the traditional mercantile elite,
or with the small new manufacturing bourgeoisie that has emerged
on the back of the international development schemes of the 1980s.
However, the mercantile elite have traditionally relied on monopoly
control of trade into and out of the country, and between the countryside and the cities, to obtain their incomes. This elite includes the
top five to ten families within the country that have almost completely
dominated Haiti's imports and few exports, primarily coffee. It has
also included the middlemen who have brought the peasant surpluses
to the towns and cities. Both these groups have not hesitated to use
the power of the state to protect their monopolies. Attempts by peasants to develop their own storage facilities and transportation networks in order to wrest control of rural extension services away from
middlemen have been met by horrific violence, perpetrated in earlier
days by the *tonton macoutes,* the militia created by François Duvalier,
and the army, and increasingly by hired muscle. It has also been widely suspected that at least some of Haiti's leading families were so
alarmed by Aristide's plans for rationalizing the economy by imposing
taxes (Haiti's elite have never paid taxes) and ending monopoly that
they backed the military coup against him.

While the traditional elite have been focused on maintaining
monopolistic practices, the new bourgeoisie have not been able to
extend their base in assembly manufacturing and ancillary services
into the rest of the economy. Profits made in this sector have not
been reinvested in building an adequate service industry in Haiti, for
instance. While political instability is partly to blame, Haitian elites
have traditionally shown a greater propensity for capitalizing the
banks of Miami and Montreal than the economy of Haiti. I vividly
remember my first day in Haiti, when the proprietor at the hotel
where I checked in instructed me to sign my travelers' checks clearly
so that the bank in Miami would not return them.

Given the limitations of the national business class, the country's
hardy peasantry could be an important source of entrepreneurial

skills. Recent international projects that have focused on bypassing middlemen to tap directly into peasant skills—the coffee growers' federation organized by the U.S. Agency for International Development (USAID), for example—have discovered that Haitian peasants are willing to work hard, cooperate, and take risks. Contrary to most popular theories that one of the reasons for Haiti's backwardness is cultural primitivism, as symbolized by the practices of *voudoun,* I would venture to state that the very lack of a clear hierarchy in *voudoun* makes its followers more prone to invention than otherwise. Unlike most of the world's organized religions, which have complex and rigid hierarchies that place both spiritual and temporal sources of authority well beyond the reach of the individual, *voudoun* suggests that all material phenomena are animated by spirits that maintain close and direct relationships with the individuals who pay obeisance to them. Individual access to these spirits is fairly easily gained, with a little help from your friendly neighborhood *houngan.* In fact, for the right price, individuals can even get spirits to do their bidding. For some, the plethora of spirits found in *voudoun* may appear to be more complex than the apparent monotheism of the semitic religions. However, in both *voudoun* and other animistic traditions, the multitude of spirits are all merely different aspects of a singular unity that underlies both spirit and matter. Hinduism's 1.5 million deities, for instance, all devolve from the same brahman. In the semitic religions, on the other hand, numerous angels, demons, and other entities appear to possess independent volition and secondary levels of power in influencing the lives of hapless humans.

The organized complexity, the heavenly multitudes, and the huge metaphysical corpus of Judaeo-Christian religions might make it easier for the cowed individual worshipper to be subjected to the long-term social and economic forces that have shaped the modern industrial democracies. The Haitian peasant, on the other hand, displays a stubborn reluctance to be subjected to social and economic engineering that could be explained by his knowledge that, secure in his mountain fastness, he is not just the master of his plot of land but also, in a manner of speaking, of his spiritual neighborhood. Control of your destiny is only a bottle of rum and a chicken sacrifice away. In fact, so pervasive are these beliefs that a leading member of Haiti's evangelical leadership argued to me that the only way to induce the kind of societal discipline that would generate rapid development in Haiti would be through firmly implanting Anglo-Saxon (presumably Judaeo-Christian and not Teutonic) values in the country.

Haitian peasant values could also be an advantage in the kinds of development strategies that do not require a Dickensian landscape of diligently and meekly toiling masses. While independent attitudes would certainly not be a desirable quality if one were looking to bring the market economy to Haiti on the back of *maquiladora* manufacturing,[41] they would definitely be a great asset in a free market system of competing peasant cooperatives and middle farmers. For those rural entrepreneurs who did not own soil fertile enough for coffee and sugarcane, access to the market could take place through handicrafts exports, even as the limited-quality soil was used for basic food production. In fact, this model has been very successfully established in a number of rural societies around the world.[42]

Throughout the nineteenth century, most conflict in Haiti resulted from urban elites struggling over government revenues. By and large, the peasantry lived in peace and modest prosperity. By the end of the nineteenth century, however, pressures on cultivable land had begun to increase tensions. The Haitian peasantry did not practice primogeniture, but instead divided land equally among their inheritors. This resulted in increasingly smaller land plots. Combined with nebulous tenure rights, this practice provided peasants with little incentive to invest in long-term conservation of soil and forest cover or to take other steps to improve productivity. With no leadership from the urban elite in investing in agricultural factors of production, Haitian agriculture began as decline as soil erosion and deforestation created land scarcity and a wider struggle for the available land. Peasant resistance to the attempts by the urban elite to tax and exploit them also increased.[43]

THE FIRST U.S. INTERVENTION

The increased instability and levels of violence, and the Chase National Bank's interests in protecting its Haitian assets, led to the first U.S. intervention in Haiti in 1915. The primary objective of the U.S. intervention was to create a viable economy in Haiti and provide a new outlet for U.S. investment. The U.S. military commanders quickly identified the light-skinned elements among the Haitian elite (in accordance with the prevalent racial attitudes at that time) as the group they could deal with, thus adding yet another unfortunate dimension to the class conflict.[44] They also attempted to force what they saw as an idle peasantry into work building roads for the new Haiti; this resulted in many clashes between the peasants and U.S. troops. The Americans also incorrectly identified excessive decentralization as a barrier to progress and created the Garde Nationale d'Haiti, which later became the Forces Armée d'Haiti (FADH), to pacify the country. They then put this instrument in the hands of their elite allies, who wielded it against the population at large.[45]

The U.S. intervention had some positive consequences. A basic infrastructure was created for Haiti. Roads and communications were expanded. Many activities that fall under the rubric of "postconflict peacebuilding" today were carried out. For the most part, however, the United States found its attempts to reshape Haiti frustrating. Mintz quotes the financial adviser to the U.S. operation, Arthur C. Millspaugh, as follows:

> The peasants, living lives which to us seem indolent and shiftless, are enviably carefree and contented; but, if they are to be citizens of an independent, self-governing nation, they must acquire, or at least a large number of them must acquire, a new set of wants.[46]

Mintz then comments on Millspaugh: "In fact, it is maddening to us, who believe that increasing one's standard of living (measured, of course, by what people buy) is a universal good, to have to confront a people who fail to share that belief... the Americans were angered and hurt by the apparent unwillingness of the Haitians to accept a North American conception of what was desirable and good." Contemporary American policymakers dealing with Haiti might experience a sense of *déja vu*. Perhaps symbolically, the contemporary visitor to Haiti might be confronted with many a potholed road that has not been repaired or rebuilt since the days of the U.S. occupation.

THE DUVALIERS

The United States left Haiti in 1934. The army it left behind continued to oppress Haitians. However, U.S.-sponsored projects also created a tiny middle class of Creole-speaking black professionals whose attitudes were at odds with those of the elite. This middle class spawned a nationalist movement called Les Griots. In 1957, riding on the back of this new movement, a certain François Duvalier became president of Haiti. Surfing the crest of *voudoun* and Creole chauvinism, Duvalier targeted the old mercantile elite and the leadership of the Catholic church. He drove many of this gentry into exile. The remnants quickly adapted to the new order, which was enforced by the nefarious Volunteers for National Security, or *tonton macoutes*. Despite his rhetoric, Duvalier was no messiah for Haiti's masses. Under his vicious rule, Haiti's economy shrank even further. Horrified by his brutal persecution of his opponents, the United

States suspended aid. The regime took no initiatives for the betterment of the masses. In fact, despite their apparent persecution, the merchants increased their share of the country's wealth. Social inequities became worse.[47]

Following his death in 1971, Duvalier was succeeded by his son, Jean-Claude Duvalier, who did not subscribe to his father's strident nationalism or his vindictiveness towards his opponents. In many ways, he appeared to be the kind of benign despot who was perceived as being a force for growth in the developing world at that time. As a result, USAID, the World Bank, and the Inter-American Development Bank sank nearly $400 million into Haiti. The vast majority of this aid was for disaster relief and agricultural development. A U.S. Congress General Accounting Office report concluded in 1982 that these programs had had little impact on Haiti's poverty.[48] The three agencies then came up with an overall growth strategy for the country. This strategy was prepared in the context of the Caribbean Basin Initiative (CBI) which was implemented in the 1980s with the primary intent of using Caribbean island states as offshore assembly platforms.

4

UNDERDEVELOPMENT IN HAITI

WRONG PREMISES, WRONG STRATEGIES

Most supporters of sustainable development have argued for the primacy of agricultural self-sufficiency in an economic development strategy for Haiti. I disagree with them, and believe that only an export-oriented strategy will bring prosperity for the majority of people. However, I also disagree with other proponents of this strategy who argue for the primacy of *maquiladora* industries. I believe that the comprehensive marketization of Haitian agriculture, conducted in accordance with local conditions, is an equally important component of sustainable export-led growth and will argue this point here and in the next chapter. Given the paucity of reliable data on Haiti, I am willing to accept that my argument could be wrong and be persuaded otherwise. Hence, I will urge the reader to see this argument as an invitation for debate, rather than a definitive statement of fact. However, I do believe that the economic strategy outlined in the following pages is the only one that can deliver equitable growth that is also *politically* feasible in the current Haitian context.

The broad international strategy for Haiti's development was based on the following premises:[49]

First, the problems in Haitian agriculture arose from excess population in the rural areas. This excess labor had to be sent to the cities, and large landowners had to convert from growing food crops to cash crops using modern technology. While Haiti would no longer be self-sufficient in food, it would make up for this deficit, and even turn a profit, through earnings from increased exports. As with the first U.S. adventure in Haiti, the idle peasantry had to be converted into an industrial labor force.

Second, once shifted to the urban areas, the excess labor would quickly be absorbed by a growing number of assembly plants assembling everything from golf balls to transistors for export to the United States. These assembly plants would capitalize on Haiti's only comparative advantage, the cheapest labor in the Caribbean, and on proximity to U.S. markets, and generate an export surplus for Haiti. This surplus would serve as the basis for further economic development.

The third element of the development formula would include a functioning government for Haiti, with a small but effective state that had privatized most functions, collected taxes, and enforced law and order. Such a state would encourage both foreign and domestic private investment.

A similar formula is now being advocated for Haiti. Between 1971 and 1991, however, this formula had been tried with only limited success, despite Haiti's being in better circumstances then than it is now. There are several assumptions in this formula that do not completely apply to the Haitian reality.

First, the formula assumed that Haiti's rural areas were occupied by idle masses who needed to be employed elsewhere. While Haiti's population and the pressure on land (largely manifested in soil erosion and scarcity of cultivable land) were increasing exponentially throughout the period from the 1960s to the 1990s, these two variables were not directly correlated. The adverse impact of population increase on land resulted not only from Malthusian dynamics, but also from new members of the rural populace turning to new land because of uncertain titles to old land, land grabs by the rural elite, an absence of investment in conserving and rehabilitating old land, and smaller (hence less productive) plots on the old land due to non-primogeniture inheritance.[50] The answer, therefore, lay perhaps not in pushing large numbers of people off the land[51] but in ensuring firmer titles; educating peasants in conservation, investment, and marketing; and encouraging them to consolidate small plots through cooperative farming (which has a very strong precursor in Haiti in the *konbite,* or collaborative rural work gangs formed in times of adversity).[52]

Second, the formula assumed that a rationalization of Haitian agriculture could only be carried out by the large landowners. The latter, however, sat on large plots of land and grabbed even more from the peasants but, with a few exceptions, did little to create an agriculture that would generate significant export earnings. Absentee landlordism remains a major obstacle in Haiti in implementing an adequate land reform program.

Third, the formula assumed that assembly manufacturing in the cities would absorb the outflow of labor from the rural areas.[53] By the time of the 1991 coup, Haiti had 60,000 workers in sweatshops—a significant figure for a country of 6 million, but small compared to levels of migration from the countryside. Prospects of city employment lured many off the land. However, the owners of the new factories did not reinvest their export earnings in the economy. In common with their rural counterparts, they put their savings in Miami bank accounts, and did little to expand production.[54] Since the masses were an enemy class, investing profits in production that would employ them was a waste of money.

Fourth, the formula assumed that the state could be reformed through such means as privatization and better tax collection. This assumption ignored the fact that the Haitian state had traditionally existed to serve the dominant classes against their own people. Furthermore, its organs also served as a battleground for contending elites. In these circumstances, the distinction between public and private was not so tightly drawn as some in the international community believed. Industrial growth in Haiti remained stunted not because the private sector was in public hands, but because all industry, public and private, was in the hands of a small elite that, for the most part, sought to serve only its own interests.[55] Additionally, following their mobilization in the 1980s, the Haitian masses saw the business elite not as a national entrepreneurial asset, but as the class enemy. Under these circumstances, all actions of the Haitian state, even reformist ones, became moves on the chessboard of class conflict. When Aristide tried to institute a progressive tax collection system in 1991, the elite, few of whom paid taxes, saw it as a blow against their interests. Similarly, President Preval's attempts to rationalize government were seen as a blow by the elite against the lower classes because of the numbers of people who would be unemployed.

Fifth, the formula assumed that the only comparative advantage Haiti enjoyed was that of cheap labor, and that the only repository of entrepreneurial skills was the elite. A recent study in the political economy of urban survival in Haiti suggested otherwise through a detailed study of the entrepreneurial skills of the masses, and of their ability to make rational decisions.[56] With appropriate credit and organization, these skills could have been mobilized far more effectively on-site than could the externally based resources of an elite which saw its own country as a danger to its prosperity. Furthermore, the relentless exploitation of labor was not the only way for Haiti to enter the world economy. The Caribbean Basin Initiative (CBI) also saw some island nations becoming offshore service platforms, particularly for the software development, tourism, and banking sectors. Many experts had attested that when the opportunities presented themselves, Haitians opted for education and technical training with a fervor that was remarkable for any society.[57] These traits, coupled with a coherent national identity, would make the country an ideal service haven. The implementation of the CBI largely ignored these aspects, not just for Haiti, but for the entire region.[58]

Sixth, the formula assumed that the export-driven development strategy could be implemented in a neutral fashion. As happens in any environment when large new resources are suddenly brought in, those best positioned to avail themselves of these resources are those who are strong to begin with. The Haitian elite quickly adapted to the new aid environment. They adopted the language of free markets and the rhetoric of order and stability, even as the Haitian state continued to be oppressively predatory. To the extent that the elite adopted this new language, they gained the attention of the international aid community with projects ostensibly designed to assist the Haitian people. However, this aid also led to a popular perception of many international agencies as actors in the class conflict rather than as neutral benefactors. After the 1991 coup, however, many international agencies reevaluated their policies in favor of more balanced actions.

SOME CONSEQUENCES

These faulty assumptions had produced disastrous consequences by the 1980s that were compounded by the famous "swine slaughter" of 1982.[59] The black pig had historically been one of the mainstays of the Haitian peasant economy. In 1978, African swine fever was detected in pigs in the Dominican Republic, and shortly thereafter in Haitian pigs. Experts deemed Haitian pigs resistant to the disease since only a tiny number were affected. However, U.S. officials declared the threat large enough to threaten the U.S. pork industry and recommended that all Haitian pigs be slaughtered and replaced by pigs from Iowa. A dependent Haitian government complied, and with the help of the USAID and the Organization of American States, it had slaughtered the majority of pigs by 1984. The sponsors of the program also decreed that only those farmers who had the ability to build the complex pigsties and buy the expensive enriched feed required by the new pigs were eligible to own them. This ruled out most Haitian peasants. Those who tried to form rural cooperatives for obtaining pigs and distributing them free were branded as communists and hunted down by the government. In any event, the new pigs proved unsuited to Haitian conditions (the old pigs had survived on garbage) and died in large numbers.

The pig slaughter sent thousands of peasants, who were already on the move due to overpopulation and the changes wrought in Haitian agriculture due to international development policies, streaming into crowded slums in the cities. By 1997, 700,000 Haitians had to be fed every year by USAID with U.S. rice. Haiti, which had been self-sufficient in food three decades previously, now imported half of its food. On the other hand, the need for new imports was not met by new agricultural exports. While the old system had been largely destroyed, it had not been replaced.

5

HAITI AFTER THE DUVALIERS

THE ARISTIDE PHENOMENON

The unemployed masses in the Haitian city slums had become a major source of tension by the mid-1980s. An additional source of tension had been the political alliances made by Jean-Claude Duvalier. While his father had used government monies to foster a nationalist elite who formed a political counterweight to the mercantile elite, Jean-Claude rebuilt alliances with the traditional bourgeoisie, who had quickly reincarnated themselves as democracy-prone entrepreneurs to take advantage of the possibilities presented by assembly industries. Tensions between the traditional Duvalierists and the new entrepreneurs in the armed forces and in the government had created enough rifts in the Duvalier regime to lead to its collapse by 1986.

All elites shared a remarkable tendency towards political bickering. Along with shifting U.S. support for various factions, this bickering led to a number of military and civilian governments following each other in rapid succession until the elections in 1990. These elections were the first free and fair elections in the history of Haiti, and would not have been possible without significant electoral assistance from the UN and the OAS. A previous attempt to hold elections in 1987 had ended with the military dictatorship slaughtering voters by the dozens.

U.S. officials backed Marc Bazin, a Western-trained technocrat with sound liberal credentials and a progressive outlook on social and economic policy, but with a political base in the Haitian elite. Opposing him was a radical priest named Jean-Bertrand Aristide, who headed a movement known as the Lavalas, or the "flood," whose political base lay in Haiti's masses. Subsequent international characterizations of his surprise victory termed the resulting Haitian government as "deeply flawed." When he was overthrown in a military coup in 1991, many expressed regret and condemned the coup, but given Aristide's "revolutionary rhetoric" and his ostensibly antibusiness policies, saw the coup as being only a matter of time. Hence, even as the international community used first sanctions and then force to oust the coup leaders, attempts were made over the three-year period that Aristide spent in exile to "mainstream" him—to get him to tone down his rhetoric and change his messianic persona. In return, he was to be reinstated as president. Aristide lived up to this Mephistophilean bargain by adopting a dual persona. Following his reinstatement, he presented himself as a liberal democrat in English and French when speaking to foreign officials, and railed against imperialism and the bourgeoisie in Creole when addressing the masses. At the time of writing in 1998, he still continued to do so.[60]

The perception of Aristide's 1990–1991 government as "flawed"[61] is not borne out by all analyses, however; a senior international official recently described the elections of 1990 to me as a "quiet revolution." For many in the international community, and for the Haitian elite, the peasantry and the newly formed urban labor force were at worst idle, and at best a *tabula rasa* on which plans for a new Haiti could be written (in fact, the existing development plans for Haiti required inert masses, as in South Korea or Taiwan during the industrialization phase). On the other hand, the Haitian peasant still saw himself as the proud inheritor of the world's only successful slave rebellion. As several experts on Haiti had determined, the Haitian peasantry, along with the migrants in the cities, had actually displayed considerably more aptitude for cooperation and entrepreneurship than had the elite.[62] This aptitude led to the remarkable phenomenon that occurred in Haiti in the post-Duvalier years, which went largely unnoticed elsewhere: the growth of a network of grassroots organizations and cooperatives at the section and village level throughout the countryside. Mobilized by Aristide's oratory, these organizations formed the backbone of the Lavalas movement. In countless villages, they faced up to the resident *tonton macoute* or *chef de section* who had represented the heavy hand of the Haitian elite. They jealously guarded the freedom and fairness of the election process in 1990. According to Amy Wilentz, writing in the critically acclaimed *The Rainy Season: Haiti Since Duvalier:*

> The priest led me through the rice cooperative, with its bags of stacked rice, and the sewing cooperative, with its two sewing machines and its neatly arrayed tables. He showed me the ironwork-

ing cooperative, scraps of metal strewn across the floor, and a forge in the corner. Last, he showed me the pigsty, where the peasants were raising new American pigs in the long cement structure, a pig apartment building where each family had its own room. "This is just like the rest of the cooperative," the priest told me while he played with a litter of grunting excited piglets. "We're doing all this together so that we don't have to rely on the old ways of doing things, so we don't have to pay off the chef de section and the local Tonton Macoute authorities, and all the old bad people. You call it 'grass roots,'" he said, pronouncing the English words awkwardly.[63]

Democracy, therefore, was a phenomenon with a strong base in Haiti. Nor was this democracy a populist upsurge of the masses. The Lavalas movement included in its ranks, apart from Aristide, intellectuals and theorists like economist and OPL leader Gerard Pierre-Charles and agronomist Rosny Smarth, the former prime minister. In many ways, these persons represented a small but significant new elite, willing to look beyond the traditional class differences and develop a truly national vision for Haiti's political and economic future.

Aristide's 1990 government saw many initial attempts to develop this vision.[64] It attempted to rationalize the tax system, collect taxes, and reduce the upper echelons of the bureaucracy. For this, it earned the wrath of the elite, who cried foul and decamped with their money. It attempted to launch education and training programs, and managed to increase foreign exchange reserves from nothing to $12 million.[65] It cut government fat in some areas. While there was some violence, it needs to be seen in the context of forward movement after centuries of oppression.[66] Attempts to end national or regional domination by traditional, regressive elites in the United States and Britain, for instance, had led to extensive civil wars. While Aristide's fiery rhetoric had been blamed by many for violence, this rhetoric might have been the only device keeping the Haitian masses engaged with their government. While Aristide had many personal and political faults—including a lurking messiah complex, inattention to policy detail, and a tendency to arrive late for meetings with international officials—an inability to govern was not among them.

Many have criticized Aristide for his speech of September 27, 1991, three days prior to his overthrow, in which he called for the elite to join a national effort of reform and renewal. He also reportedly urged the masses to resort to harsher measures if the popular will was thwarted, and to vigilante measures such as *pere lebrun*, or "necklacing" with burning tires, if they were attacked. Some who heard the speech said that, as with so much of his vivid imagery, he was using *pere lebrun* as a metaphor for a radical change or cleansing. Credible independent evidence suggests that Aristide was speaking not so much on the basis of a whimsical desire to see Haiti's elite "necklaced" but in response to reports of the impending coup. The *pere lebrun* imagery was therefore intended to warn away prospective coup plotters by invoking the potential wrath of the people against a violent overthrow of an elected government.[67]

CONSEQUENCES OF THE COUP

The 1991 coup, and the resulting international sanctions, had several detrimental consequences. With Haiti unable to export, many of the assembly manufacturers left. This worsened the unemployment problem, and made the urban masses even more restive. The military rulers now had greater leeway in targeting the network of prodemocracy organizations that had made the 1990 elections a success. Despite the valiant but ineffective efforts of MICIVIH, the joint United Nations / Organization of American States human rights monitoring mission, the military proceeded unimpeded to liquidate the leadership and much of the membership of grassroots organizations.[68] More than three thousand prodemocracy activists were brutally killed. In many rural districts, tyrannical officials who had been ousted by these activists returned to maim and oppress. Much of this work was done by a militia called Fronte Révolutionnaire pour l'Avancement et le Progrès en Haiti (FRAPH), headed by Emmanuel Constant.

A further important outcome of the coup and the embargo was the increased role that largely U.S.-based nongovernmental organizations (NGOs) came to play in Haiti. Organizations such as CARE and the Pan-American Development Foundation were entrusted with administering USAID programs through the 1980s. The rationale was an ineffective Haitian state. During the coup years, when contacts with the illegal government were forbidden, NGOs became the primary vehicle for disbursing international assistance in Haiti. What was remarkable about this NGO activity in Haiti was the level of agreement among both independent analysts and the primary targets of this activity—the Haitians themselves—about the extent to which it had aided in the disruption of local economic activity, particularly by creating dependency among the peasants and by preventing the development of local institutions for sustainable development. A summary of a 1997 Grassroots International report provided by the

Washington Office on Haiti quoted Haitian senator Samuel Madisten as follows:

> CARE has been "helping" people in the Northwest for decades. But each year, the misery of the people of the Northwest increases. What is the real impact of this aid? To make people more dependent, more vulnerable, more on the margins?...The aid is not given in such a way as to give the people responsibility, to make the people more independent.... This is what you call "commercializing" poverty.... The people's misery should not be marketed....[69]

An extensive opinion survey by Grassroots International of the purported beneficiaries of international aid offered such conclusions as these:

> The U.S.-based NGOs that carry out most USAID programs do not adequately consult or coordinate with local, regional, and Haitian government authorities, ... often bypass relevant Haitian governmental entities, often putting resulting development projects at odds with stated national, regional, and local priorities.... Private aid agencies consistently operated jobs-creation programs in rural areas at key planting and harvesting times, pulling people out of their fields with the lure of relatively high short-term wages.... USAID-funded programs stifle local initiative with short-term offers of free food and employment, creating cycles of dependency among Haitian farmers.... Private aid agencies frequently fail to consult or work with local community organizations; instead they either directly implement projects themselves or work closely with discredited local elites.[70]

While these conclusions can be faulted on the grounds of the overall policy positions of the organizations that have produced them, many UN officials in Haiti had also expressed to me, in their unofficial capacity, their frustration over the negative impact of international NGOs on local governance.

Overall, the most critical impact of the coup period was seriously to undermine the community-level infrastructure that had generated a 80 percent voter turnout in the 1990 elections. Furthermore, the decline of this infrastructure also undermined the links that had been built between the progressive bourgeoisie and the masses under the Lavalas umbrella. The fact that the maximum voter turnout in elections backed by the international community since 1994 had never exceeded 40 percent, and the tense overtones of class conflict that characterized Haitian politics at the time of writing, could be attributed to this decline.

By the late 1990s, the most visible aspect of Haiti's problems remained the mistrust between the elite and the masses. It is important to stress here that development policies pursued in Haiti since the 1980s greatly exacerbated class tensions. Masses of angry youth in the cities gave Aristide's rhetoric in his first term a far sharper edge than would otherwise have been the case. These youths often participated in violent acts that threatened to fray the alliance between a tiny group of progressive bourgeoisie and the masses under the Lavalas umbrella. The elites responded in an equally radical fashion. Their fears of literal extermination helped produce both the coup and the extreme measures of the coup authorities. The continuation of previously unsuccessful development strategies continued to exacerbate class tensions in Haiti after the coup. According to Grassroots International, "such development strategies are threatening to undermine Haiti's chance to build democracy by driving a wedge between the government of President René Preval and the Haitian people."[71]

By 1994, the flow of refugees fleeing the gratuitous violence of the military regime had seriously jeopardized the Democratic Party's political fortunes in Florida and brought the Haitian diaspora onto the streets of Brooklyn and Miami demanding political action. Resulting political pressures prompted a U.S.-led military intervention to staunch the flow of refugees.

The long-term impact of the MNF-led invasion was smaller than it could have been. The most significant measure undertaken by U.S. troops—the arrest of the military attachés who had perpetrated the most violence—was reversed shortly thereafter. The release of these individuals, and the failure of a weapons buy-back program, might have resulted in a continuation of occasional violent attacks by the far right on community organizations in Haitian villages and slums. To give it credit, the MNF did establish quite clearly, through a fire fight in which several right-wing thugs were killed, that the United States would not tolerate gratuitous violence from the far-right elements, since such violence produced refugees. MNF patrols also greatly increased overall security in the villages and towns. And through the creation of an Interim Public Security Force, the MNF facilitated the disbanding of the murderous FADH and the establishment of the Haitian National Police.[72] In 1995, this burden of providing security was taken up by the United Nations.

6

RECOMMENDATIONS FOR PEACEBUILDING

From the discussion so far, the following could be suggested as Haiti's critical needs: a process of reconciliation that creates a consensual strategy for Haiti's economic and political development; the creation of constitutional order, and of rule of law, where class and other conflicts are managed through capable institutions rather than through conflict and vendetta; and a serious reconsideration of the development policies that have been adopted for Haiti.

NATIONAL RECONCILIATION

As mentioned earlier, before the coup Lavalas had included a coalition of the enlightened bourgeoisie and leaders of community organizations. This coalition had come under severe stress as the OPL faction had taken the position that President Aristide should not run for a second consecutive term despite his great personal popularity. To the extent that Aristide had not fully cooperated with the government that succeeded him, OPL leaders said that he was now attempting to use charisma and personality-based politics to win his way back to power instead of working within a stable institutional context. The alleged attempts by Haiti's Provisional Electoral Council—supposedly dominated by Aristide supporters—to use irregular means to sway the results in Aristide's favor were seen as another example of this power grab. Aristide's Famille Lavalas, on the other hand, had taken the position that the institutionalization agenda and the accompanying free market reforms that OPL deemed essential constituted only superficial democracy, which did nothing to address the critical needs of Haiti's masses. Aristide had also complained that the new elite remained as aloof from the masses as did the old elite, rarely bothering to communicate with them and not responding to their concerns.

The standoff between OPL and Aristide had negated one significant element that had characterized the old Lavalas movement—its ability to bridge the gap between the masses and the progressive members of the elite. Newly liberated countries need national organizations and movements—like the Congress in India and the ANC in South Africa—at crucial moments in their history to bridge fundamental divides among their peoples. While these countries had had elections, their politics had initially been dominated by national unity governments in the interests of ensuring both participation and unity. Where they had succeeded in stabilizing their countries, these movements had included two components: a charismatic leadership capable of mobilizing the masses to forgive the hatreds of the past, to swallow tough economic medicine, and to make sacrifices for their country; and a group of capable technocrats who were able to mobilize resources and implement strategies.

In Haiti, however, the charismatic leaders and the technocrats had split from each other. Unfortunately, this split had also taken on a class dimension along age-old lines. The OPL and its political allies, reflecting the bourgeois fear of the tyranny of the masses, remained doubtful of Aristide's democratic intentions. Mass opinion, on the other hand, was increasingly dismissive of the elite as having only its own interests at heart, in accordance with tradition. These perceptions were unfortunate, because Haiti needed both economic reform and those who could sell it to the people; it needed not just the resources of the elite but also the participation of the masses. Furthermore, the international community, having vigorously expressed its preferences, was seen as being a player in this conflict on the side of the elite. International pronouncements on Haiti became suspect. For instance, a senior Haitian official with progressive credentials suggested to me in late 1997 that in order for the crucial parliamentary elections scheduled for November 1998 to be successful, they would need to be monitored by agencies other than the traditional monitors: the UN, the United States, and the OAS.

This situation was compounded by the fact that the international community had applied to Haiti a methodology for peace support operations that had been developed elsewhere. This methodology was characterized by benchmarks by which international officials could claim to have restored a country to good health. All international interventions were seen as needing an "exit policy" and benchmarks for the implementation of this policy.[73] On the political front, these benchmarks were usually elections, and an elected government that could be recognized as legitimate. Since the "exit policy" needed to have a shorter, rather than a longer, time-frame, these benchmarks had to be realized within a limited period of time. Expensive elections and other democracy-building exercises were, therefore, conducted in several conflicted societies not on the basis of any local rationale, but in order to "exit" quickly. While elections were not the primary goal of international interventions, as recent critiques have mistakenly suggested, they definitely became one of the primary means for achieving international goals. However, in many instances, the need of the hour was further reconciliation and power-sharing rather than a quick election that reinforced conflict through a simple majority dynamic. In Haiti, the emphasis on implementing this standardized *modus operandi* might have reinforced the formation of political groups along class lines, the advent of knee-jerk populism instead of rational policy, and a weak government constantly strung out on the horns of political bickering.

While the post-1994 process of government was legitimate, it was by no means adequate. Haiti was a developing country undergoing extremely rapid and very fundamental change. Unlike developed countries, it did not have the luxury to wait for fundamental differences or concerns over economic and other policies to be sorted out only via elections every five years. Through such means as multiparty dialogues, forums, and joint commissions targeted at specific and substantive issues, the political process in Haiti needed to be continuously augmented and made more timely and representative. While fair and free elections would be the only means through which a government was constituted in Haiti, for now even an elected government would have to function in some areas as a government of national unity. The South African and the Guatemalan models could serve as examples.

An equally critical aspect of reconciliation was justice. Steps needed to be taken to target the particularly horrendous abuses committed by the military and the FRAPH. In fact, the gratuitous nature of these abuses had brought together an extremely diverse expatriate Haitian community, including members of all classes, and sent them out into the streets of New York and Miami to demand democracy.[74] Subsequently, however, many in Haiti's slums and streets had branded the entire elite as guilty for the lapses of the military regime. Instead of seeing individuals who need to be punished for their crimes, an entire class was branded as "macoutes" or "putschists." Furthermore, the release of many criminals shortly after they were apprehended by U.S. Special Forces created an atmosphere where many Haitians believed that elements of the military regime were still around to target activists. Following Aristide's restoration in 1994, a complete and transparent accounting of political crimes should have occurred. Instead, a Haitian government commission was formed with international assistance, and with no powers, to prepare a voluminous report on the crimes. This report was never circulated broadly and resulted in no prosecutions, no arrests, no trials, or not even one instance where a criminal member of the previous regime offered a public apology.[75]

These unfortunate developments left many Haitians with a tremendous sense of unaddressed grievance that manifested itself in renewed class warfare; this prevented the emergence of a truly national ruling class with the ability to mobilize the sweat and tears of common Haitians on behalf of national development. Instead, the elite was seen as being corrupt, self-serving, or in the pockets of the *macoutes* or the foreigners by most of the masses, and therefore as unworthy of demanding any sacrifices. These unfortunate perceptions did not do justice to those members of the elite, and of the Haitian diaspora, who were willing to invest and save for their country.

Obviously, no ruling elite could give its people immediate deliverance from centuries of suffering. Yet, throughout history, common people have shown great resilience and willingness to sacrifice when motivated by enough hope and by a truly transcendent purpose. Of Haiti's political leadership, only Aristide was able to communicate with the masses in Creole, with the appropriate inflections and metaphors. Therefore, a process of government that would have at least provided the appearance of engaging the population in the development process at every level of representation was critically needed. Instead, an ineffective government was seen as working with international aid agencies to undercut local representatives at the district and village level. The World Bank had eventually started inviting local NGOs and officials to meetings to discuss economic strategy for Haiti. These meetings were deemed a great success. By all accounts, they also had very little impact on popular perceptions of the government. One explanation could be that they reached only those Haitians who were already in the best position to communicate with, and benefit from, international involvement in Haiti. The challenge, therefore, was to identify a broader constituency of aid recipients and intermediaries who could effectively communicate the purposes and planning behind international activities in Haiti to the common people, and who could work with the international community in developing a more effective system for the delivery of aid to the target sectors.

CONSTITUTIONAL ORDER AND THE RULE OF LAW

The primary factor in the establishment of institutional stability in Haiti was seen by the international community as being the Haitian National Police. However, the force was held in contempt by many on both the left and the right. For the left it was seen as an instrument of oppression for the bourgeoisie and for the international "occupation," who wanted to force Haitians into *maquiladora* factories. For the right, it was an inefficient nonentity that could not guarantee the safety of the elite; they openly longed for the army and considered its abolishment a mistake. In many ways, these criticisms had made the police a symbol of the international community's sometimes quixotic search for a middle ground where none existed. The criticisms also reflected a bigger problem in the logic of making the police force the focus of peacebuilding efforts. While many saw the force as the causal variable behind institutional stability, another possibility could be that both institutional stability and a successful police force resulted from a third variable—national political reconciliation. As long as the Haitian leadership continued to be divided along class lines, all initiatives, no matter how worthy, would be seen as favoring one group or another. In the absence of a national understanding of what was good for Haiti, instead of the interests of one group being represented as the national interest, even a neutral police force was seen as enforcing the interests of a small elite or not doing enough to curb populist violence. Hence, in the absence of a concerted effort to create such understanding, any police force, no matter how neutral, would have been little more than a Band-Aid.

In the short term, the international community could have taken some additional measures to ensure that the police force had the trust and confidence of the population. The most critical would have been a viable justice system. Courts and judges that were willing to apply the law equally to all Haitians, and deal with disputes that caused some of the greatest amount of recrimination among the classes such as land disputes, were desperately needed in Haiti at the time of writing. Despite years of international effort, no such system existed. Reasons for this are difficult to come by. An NGO staff member with long experience told me that the management of justice programs implemented by international agencies in Haiti was deeply flawed. Project managers had either no relevant technical skills or lacked appropriate country experience. A more fundamental factor could have been that many among Haiti's elites, long used to pliable magistrates, were not interested in an independent judiciary. Furthermore, despite the impressive efforts of certain peacekeeping contingents to repair prisons in their spare time, Haiti also remained without a viable prison system. Little effort appeared to have been made to tap into local resources and assess local priorities for building a responsive justice system.

An important step in building a viable police force would have been to build it from the ground up. In most open societies, a centralized police force would be an anachronism. In the Haiti of the past, the centralized force created by the United States during its first intervention in Haiti became the primary instrument for dictatorship. This was because policing was essentially a community function. In Haiti particularly, the potential for the misuse of a centralized force, no matter how well trained or how neutral, would remain high. In these circumstances, a better strategy would have been to facilitate the formation of a network of community police organizations that functioned independently, but with a leadership that had been through common training at a centralized academy. In this system, the police would function closely in accordance with the priorities established by elected local representatives, irrespective of the class group from which this leadership emerged. In fact, until a formal nationwide system for justice could be created, local councils could combine the functions of administration, justice, and security, in the manner that the *panchayati raj* system does at the village level in India, for instance.[76] This system would have gone a long way towards addressing the growing problems of drug-related and gang violence that plagued Haiti's communities. It was partly in recognition of the importance of the community aspects of policing that Canadian peacekeepers in Haiti had instituted several programs for building police-community relations. Also, given the tensions that prevailed in some localities between those accused of being *macoutes* and the Lavalas activists, the building of common community police structures could have been used as an important reconciliation and confidence-building measure.

ECONOMIC DEVELOPMENT

The following could be suggested as remedial measures for Haiti's problems of economic development:

First, *a reassessment needs to be carried out of the potential of Haiti's peasantry.* Despite direct attacks by Haiti's elite and by U.S. forces in the first half of this century, and the constant attrition of its resource base in the second half, the Haitian peasantry possesses great entrepreneurial vitality. It constitutes an asset, and not a burden, in terms of deepening and institutionalizing the market economy in Haiti. The problems of the small scale of peasant agriculture that had been considered an obstacle to modernization could be easily overcome through the creation of cooperatives, a form of organization to which Haitian peasants appeared remarkably prone. The monopoly that has been exercised by middlemen in getting the peasants' produce to the market could be checked through providing some minimal infrastructure and education through which peasants themselves could get their produce to the market. In a trip to the Haitian Northeast during 1996, I saw the difference that a small gravel road (the Limonade road project built by Pakistani peacekeepers) had made in the fortunes of the village next to it. In Fond Jean-Noel, a USAID project had constituted a federation of 18,000 farmers into twenty-five cooperatives to grow and market the increasingly popular Haitian Bleu coffee for export to U.S. markets, without the traditional middlemen.[77] Given the direct involvement of peasants in this project, and the fact that the coffee bush required the shade of large trees, many project participants had taken to actively conserving trees instead of felling them.[78] These projects pointed to the possibility of tapping into the natural talents of the Haitian peasant.[79]

Land reform remains critical to agricultural development. In the minds of many in both Haiti and the United States, the issue of land reform conjures up French Revolution–type images of mindless peasants running to grab land and massacring landowners. Yet most farmers appear ready to go through due process in obtaining land. According to one estimate, claims filed for tenure in the Artibonite Valley twice exceeded the total landmass of Haiti. The missing element here was a judicial system to address these claims. Given the fact that Haiti did not seem close to having this system in the short run, the best strategy would have been to encourage alternate, local forms of arbitration.

Food security is another critical issue, and a deliberately politicized one. Many Haitians argue that the pressure to eliminate all tariffs would sound the death knell for Haitian agriculture, particularly rice cultivation. This argument is incomplete. In a free market environment, Haiti should be able to export coffee and other cash crops, and then pay for rice imports, and turn a greater investable profit than would be realized from rice cultivation; this process should not sound the death knell for agriculture. The problem, of course, is to reform Haitian agriculture so that it could produce for export without ruining the peasants. Projects like the USAID project at Fond Jean-Noel demonstrate that export agriculture and peasant prosperity are not necessarily incompatible. Additionally, while steps are taken to develop such projects, Haiti definitely deserves a break from the incessant demands from abroad to reduce tariffs. No one placed such demands on the United States, Britain, South Korea, or Thailand when they modernized agriculture. Haiti also needs a break from the ostensibly humanitarian activities of those international NGOs that disrupt agriculture through ill-conceived projects or who allow food to be dumped in the guise of relief.

Second, *Haiti needs a different industrial strategy.*[80] At the time of writing, the experience of H. H. Cutler, Disney's primary subcontractor in Haiti, had demonstrated the limits of *maqiladora*-led industrialization. Under pressure for paying its workers only 56 cents an hour, H. H. Cutler decided to fire its 2,300 employees and move to Indonesia (where workers toiled for an even more miserable wage of 13 cents an hour but did not suffer from the travails of democracy or from the inflation-creating slush money of nonresident elites). Clearly, H. H. Cutler was strictly focused on short-term profit. In fact, there is not much evidence that *maquiladora* activities have resulted in a long-term process of capital generation and investment in the Haitian economy. What other economic possibilities exist?

New small- and medium-scale economic enterprises should be developed, particularly in the areas of tourism, services, and handicrafts. One area that could produce a windfall for Haiti is tourism. Despite ecological disaster in the highlands, Haiti still has some of the world's most beautiful beaches and coastlines. Tapping into this potential requires not an isolated Club Med but a sustained partnership with the Haitian people. Cooperative promotion of tourism, in alliance with local communities, could be used to promote the kind of eco-tourism that is increasingly popular with Western middle classes tired of the usual circuit of Holiday Inns and two-hour cruise stops.[81] Haiti's cultural vibrancy, coupled with the extensive decency that the average Haitian displays towards foreigners, could be major assets. In fact, Haitian art alone, if marketed well, could produce impressive profits. Given its small size, Haiti produces a prodigious amount of hauntingly beautiful visual art and music, with overtones of the mystical, that is often sold for a pittance. This art is one of Haiti's greatest assets.

Another asset is native Haitian intelligence. Given the opportunity, many Haitians show a remarkable proclivity for such professions as banking and medicine. They are heavily inclined towards education. Even the poorest families dress their children in clean uniforms each morning to go schools that often lack basic facilities. Once surrounded by an enabling environment, Haitians could perform remarkably well in exacting professions. The key to tapping into this talent is not unskilled wage labor, but education, as suggested by Ericq Pierre, Haiti's director on the Inter-American Development Bank. In his *The Third Wave*, Alvin Toffler had argued that agricultural societies could bypass the industrial phase and jump directly to the information age. Data processing and software development require modest amounts of electricity and infrastructure and lots of education, but not steel mills or *maquiladora* factories. Haiti could be an offshore platform for labor-intensive software development, for instance, rather than for labor-intensive baseball knitting. Not far from the bed-and-breakfast where I stayed in Haiti in the winter of 1997, a "Compuworld cyber-cafe" offered good coffee and Internet access as a small reminder of Haiti's potential.

The capital for small-scale and medium enterprises in the areas of tourism, services such as software development, and handicrafts will not come entirely from outside investors. External resources rarely act as the primary instrument for creating the first comprehensive dynamic of savings, investment, and growth in a society. An obvious source would be the nearly 1.5 million Haitians who live outside Haiti in the rest of the Americas. A concerted effort should be made to foster a relationship between the diaspora and the Haitian leadership, to provide guarantees for diaspora investment or to provide information on investment opportunities. Members of the diaspora have not been encouraged to set up funds to create, for instance, a network of technical schools that could train Haitians in managing tourism and small businesses, or software development.

BRINGING HAITI INTO THE MARKET ECONOMY

At this point, one can conduct a brief gedankenexperiment, from the U.S. perspective, to explore Haiti's prospects if an alternate macroeconomic strategy were adopted for the country. Let us assume that the primary U.S. business interest in Haiti is to be able to relocate industry to Haiti because of lower costs. What would be the best strategy to employ towards this objective? To begin with, a successful strategy would not treat the Haitian peasant as being redundant in any industrialization process. According to Trouillot:

> The light industry strategy was destined to misfire primarily because it ignored the impasse posed by the relations of production in the agrarian world. The crisis inherited by François Duvalier and exacerbated by his regime and that of his son had its roots in the contradictions of a peasant country ruled by an unholy alliance of merchants and political profiteers, an alliance cemented by the state. By

ignoring the problems of the rural world and the relationship
between it and the urban classes, the light industry strategy in the
end complicated them.[82]

Trouillot's point is well taken. As we have seen above, there had
been no indigenous dynamic of savings and reinvestment in agriculture—still the primary economic activity, despite nearly two decades
of migration from rural and urban areas. Most Haitians are still peasants, and Haitian culture and society revolve around peasant traditions. Haiti's recent development strategies have not converted these
peasants into industrial workers. Instead they have lured large numbers of peasants into towns without giving them employment, thus
leading to slums like Cité Soleil and the accompanying violence and
tensions.

A sustainable strategy would have involved the reform of Haitian
agriculture to generate a local dynamic of growth. The first step
would have been a rationalization of land tenure. Given the dominant position of a network of *chefs de section* and *tonton macoutes* in
rural society, any process of land tenure reform would have required
some pressure from the state to protect it. In the absence of a national judicial system to arbitrate this process, the considerable local presence of both the Catholic church and the *voudoun* networks might
have been used to create a de facto arbitration system. A similar
model of local governance can be found in the *panchayati raj* system
in India, where eclectic village councils combine both policing and
arbitration functions.[83]

The second critical step would have been to reorganize production so that surpluses were invested in improving local infrastructure,
generating more growth. On the landowners' side, this would have
involved some pressure to move beyond luxury consumption to
increasing production for the market. On the side of the smallhold-
ers, this step would have involved encouraging the spread of village
cooperatives to farm small plots of land together and to increase both
collective landholding and production through reinvesting profits.
Haitian peasants often form farming cooperatives that pool labor,
land, and profits into collective enterprises. International assistance
should therefore have encouraged village cooperatives to become
viable commercial enterprises.

This rationalization of Haitian agriculture would have created
both a broader tax base and an internal market for Haiti and, hence,
surpluses that could be reinvested in infrastructure. International
support for progressive elites would have greatly contributed towards
ensuring that the surpluses would be reinvested in the economy, and

not just directed to luxury consumption. Investment in infrastructure—roads and education being the most critical—would have speeded up the flow of goods between urban and rural areas; it would have both expanded the domestic market and created exportable surpluses. Additionally, government monies would have been better spent in encouraging domestic capitalization in sectors such as information services, banking, and tourism—areas in which Haitians have recently shown great facility when given the opportunity. This would have been the most appropriate time for the Haitian government to open up the internal market to foreign investors, including those interested in assembly manufacture.

The *maquiladora* investors would have encountered a far smaller pool of destitute, slum-dwelling Haitian peasants than was recently the case. Hence they would have had to pay slightly higher wages. But the overall cost of paying marginally higher wages would have been lower than numerous other benefits. In recently modernized developing countries, strong domestic markets—not to mention a good internal infrastructure—are a great boon for foreign investors of all stripes, even those who are primarily interested in cheap labor. Cheaply assembled goods can be sold domestically in ever larger numbers, thus saving some of the transport costs entailed in a scenario where these goods can only be exported. But the greatest boon comes in the form of better social relations.

If Haiti had actually focused on reforming domestic agriculture and building the prerequisites of a domestic market (as Taiwan and South Korea did in their first two decades of development) before inviting *maquiladora* investment, Haitians would have had many more options for employment than sweatshops. However, there would still have been labor available for sweatshops for those foreign investors who were interested in them. The trickle of peasants fleeing environmental degradation and land conflicts would not have been so big as after gratuitous episodes such as the pig slaughter, but would nonetheless still have existed. Many of the migrants would have had to make a beginning in the sweatshops before moving on elsewhere. Yet the presence of other areas of economic activity that added more value locally would have created a sense of forward movement and growth that would perhaps have pre-empted the clashes between labor and *maquiladora* owners that characterize contemporary Haiti. Much of the turbulence that has afflicted Haiti since 1986 would probably not have happened, and many of the *maquiladora* owners who had to leave consequently would still be there.

In rapidly developing countries such as South Korea and China, economies accommodate both software programming and assembly manufacturing. The two are not necessarily contradictory within the bounds of the same economy, and service the needs of a labor force in a state of flux as far as overall levels of skills and education are concerned. The mistake of the economic planners who developed Haiti's economic strategy during the 1980s was perhaps to assume that the only way to make Haiti a viable assembly platform for American manufacturers was to ensure that it became nothing else.

These mistakes can be corrected. The economic strategy identified above can still be implemented, if the political prerequisites are in place. The United States should push for a genuine free market in Haiti that is tempered by consensus and the rule of law, is devoid of monopoly, and benefits all Haitians.

SUSTAINABLE CONFLICT MANAGEMENT IN HAITI

At the beginning of this paper, I identified the crucial prerequisite for the building of lasting peace in Haiti as a genuine and frank consensus on the future, rooted in a continuous process of dialogue and reconciliation, between the country's various sectors and political tendencies. This consensus would provide the basis for a self-perpetuating cycle of peaceful discussion and debate within Haiti that would be the optimal longer-term conflict management mechanism for the country. It would be critical for this consensus to result from a truly national process of argument and debate involving all sectors and all levels of sociopolitical organization. To the extent that the *mounn andeyo* would not just be tolerated in this exercise, but in fact be at the center of the stage, this process would have to be inherently democratic and participatory. In the longer term, this culture of participation and accommodation would go much further in creating the civic culture required for democracy than any short-term doctrinaire insistence by the international community on the structural forms of democracy.

Fareed Zakaria has argued for "constitutional liberalism"—rule of law, respect for minorities, tolerance of diversity—as the bedrock of "liberal democracy."[84] Zakaria does not, however, delve into the historical circumstances that facilitate the emergence of constitutional liberalism. In his classic *Social Origins of Dictatorship and Democracy,* Barrington Moore argues for the emergence of economic elites that can balance the traditional feudal sectors before stable democracy emerges.[85] Indeed, the histories of all early developers reveal critical moments where some decidedly unconstitutional episodes allowed progressive elites to emerge from under those who would have stood against liberal values. The English civil war, the French revolution, and the American civil war are examples. Germany and Japan went through the bloodletting of two world wars before *junker* and *samurai* values found their place in history.

An alternate, less violent, *modus operandi* has involved national compacts through which coalitions of progressive elites have sought to weave the traditional and the modern into a shaky but nonetheless perceptibly democratic system. Usually, these compacts have taken the form of national movements. The Indian National Congress and the South African African National Congress have already been mentioned in this regard. In this context, a critical moment in modern Haitian history was the National Congress of Democratic Movements of 1987, where Haitians had gathered to discuss a new post-Duvalier constitution. Wilentz accurately captured the mood of the Congress:

> The Congress was held in a huge meeting hall run by the Salesian order, and went on each day until deep into the night. Meetings began indoors, and afterward, workshops were held out on the grounds, under the stars. Famous Port-au-Prince lawyers listened as peasants spoke about how country people could inject their ideas into the new Constitution. School teachers and priests who had left the Church railed against the human rights abuses that had been committed by General Namphy and his army. Rich mulattos sat on the dais with choir girls from the slums. The diaspora was present in scores ... exiles returned from Paris, the Dominican Republic, Venezuela, New York ... future presidential candidates, priests, nuns and pastors, Duvalier's former political prisoners, houngans, musicians, agronomists, doctors, lawyers.... Aristide sent some of his people over....[86]

This Congress supported the 1987 Constitution and a Provisional Electoral Council to conduct the next national elections. The Congress participants fielded Gerard Gorgue as their candidate for these elections. The Namphy dictatorship promised to allow the elections to proceed and continued to receive strong U.S. support. Many participants in the Congress, including Aristide, feared Namphy's intentions. Some called for delaying the elections until prodemocracy activists had had time to strengthen themselves. Others called for stronger international opposition to the human rights violations of the Namphy dictatorship. However, a senior U.S. official dealing with Central American affairs pronounced that Namphy was Haiti's "best chance for democracy." Despite that fact that a presidential candidate was assassinated by plainclothes policemen who were caught on tape killing him, U.S. officials erroneously concluded that the government had "contributed importantly to laying the groundwork for a new, more democratic Haiti."[87] When elections came around and it looked as if Gerard Gorgue might win, the Namphy dictatorship went berserk. It slaughtered voters by the dozen as they gathered to vote. Wilentz visited the site of one such massacre by army soldiers:

> The worst killings had come in the classroom opposite the voting place.... you could see the story of the massacre in the design of blood on the floor and walls. You could see them run, fall, rise, and stumble to their end. Shoes and bags and briefcases and hats stood like landmarks at the important twists and turns of futile paths. Between the lakes of blood were thin trails, drying rivers of deep red that marked the last, short movements of the dead, and then bloody tributaries winding away. It was like a map of Haiti.[88]

A chance to alter this map was lost when Namphy massacred voters and annulled the elections. Events might have taken a different course if the international community had offered strong and unqualified support for the Congress of National Democratic Movements and condemned and boycotted the Namphy dictatorship for its human rights violations in the period leading to the elections.

A similar moment was again lost with the coup against Aristide in 1991. At the present time, however, the international intervention and the dismantling of the Haitian army has created yet another opportunity to recover the lost opportunities of 1987 and 1990. Despite plenty of armed groups and weapons in Haiti, the capacity to inflict violence is more evenly distributed. No one group is capable of violently inflicting its will on all others. Under these circumstances, a new dialogue among the different sectors in Haiti—business, peasantry, students, labor, politicians—on developing a common agenda for progressive economic and political change would go a long way towards creating the kind of willingness to abide by rules for each others' sake and to tolerate each other that constitutes the "liberal" ethos seen by Zakaria and others as critical for a stable democracy.[89] This dialogue would perhaps have to be initiated on an independent platform by a neutral actor, with a more positive and overt intervention on behalf of the progressive forces by the international community at a later stage.

In recent years, the "national conference" method has been used to create a consensus of this nature in some countries in francophone Africa. In this method, the government and the leaders of the various sectors participate in a continuous session of dialogue lasting several weeks during which sovereignty is transferred from the government to the chairmanship of the conference. The conference usually develops a new constitution and a new system of government based on a truly national consensus. There is no guarantee that the ruling authorities will accept the conference's work. For instance, while Mathieu Kerekou in Benin accepted the conference, Mobutu Sese Seko in Zaire first attempted to manipulate the conference and then rejected it, thus ensuring his own violent overthrow a few years later. The "national conference" model would not be suitable for Haiti, however, for the following reasons:

First, Haiti is currently too divided to be able to settle amicably on who should participate in such a conference. When certain opposition leaders, who admittedly have far less popular standing than either of the two primary Lavalas factions, suggested a "national conference" for Haiti, most Lavalas officials responded by accusing these leaders of trying to gain through other means the power that they had not been able to obtain through the ballot box.

Second, if Haiti were to follow the model of some countries and elect delegates to a national conference, the logistics for organizing such a conference would become next to impossible. In its current state, Haiti can barely organize the elections that are already scheduled. Additionally, the current Haitian Constitution, which was itself supported by a Congress of National Democratic Movements, would probably have to be amended in order to allow a national conference delegation to be elected.

Third, Haiti has a legitimate government that, however imperfectly, has been elected in a free and fair elections. It is much more difficult to make a convincing argument for a government of this nature to hand over sovereignty to the chairmanship of a national conference than it is for a dictatorship or a one-party state.

Given these limitations on the national conference idea, the most promising alternative for Haiti's is a process similar to the one followed in Guatemala, where leaders of civil society and of the political elite have engaged in a continuous dialogue with a sovereign government for nearly half a decade as a prelude to the national negotiation that finally ended the country's civil war. Since there is no civil war to end in Haiti, a dialogue process of this nature would be targeted at developing a workable national consensus that could then guide policymaking by the executive and legislative branches of the government. Should not Haiti's elected parliament be the venue for such a dialogue? Unfortunately, in the absence of a working national consensus, both chambers of Haiti's elected parliament have become a mirror for the kind of division and acrimony that characterizes the wider polity and society.

This dialogue would also not substitute for or supplant the existing electoral process in Haiti. Similar discussions in South Africa and Guatemala recently, for example, have strengthened electoral processes rather than undermining them. The dialogue would explore ways in which mass participation in the process of governance could be brought about without creating fears of mob violence on the part of the elite, and the manner in which elite resources and skills could be tapped into without pandering to those who would create a permanent privileged class at the expense of the majority.[90] By addressing the primary fears of both elite as well as mass organizations, this dialogue might open the doors for a more constructive engagement between all sectors.

SOME LESSONS FOR PEACEBUILDING

The Haitian experience offers some useful perspectives on peacebuilding activities conducted by the international community:

First, in any scenario involving international attempts to build internal peace, the concept of the international community's neutrality is highly misleading. Through their very presence on the ground, and through the resources that they bring to bear upon their various initiatives, international actors will often irrevocably alter the local balance of forces. In the process, they will make both enemies and friends. To the extent that international officials will make choices on how conflict can be prevented in a society, they will also implant their perspectives on what is right and what is wrong within that country. Quite often, these perspectives might become a bone of contention in an internal contest for legitimacy, as happened with the UN's pronouncements on the April 1997 elections, for instance. The trick, therefore, is to ensure that the balance is altered in favor of progress and stability, and not renewed chaos and conflict. Being cognizant of the full impact of one's actions is perhaps the biggest step that international actors can take in this regard.

Second, peacebuilding is fundamentally not the responsibility of the international community, but of the parties that have to live with that peace. No process for sustainably managing conflict in a society can be imposed entirely from the top. In Haiti, the average person has little interest or say in the debates over institutionalization or the "neoliberal" economic policy that lie at the heart of international activities. Given a lack of engagement, or any manifest benefits or change in his life, that person is not just unresponsive but also feels betrayed and therefore hostile. Haiti provides a clear lesson that strategies for successful postconflict peacebuilding cannot be designed in New York or in capital cities alone.

Third, Haiti also demonstrates that local involvement in peacebuilding need not be limited to the elites. Quite often, it is the almost complete inability of the elites to move beyond their own mutual bickering and rivalries that is the primary cause of conflict in a society. Because they are closer to ground-level realities of the suffering caused by conflict and violence, it is common persons who often have the highest stake in peace. The involvement of independent civic organizations, of progressive groups, and voluntary organizations therefore becomes critical in developing a peacebuilding strategy that generates a positive longer-term impact.

Finally, peacebuilding cannot happen unless all key domestic and foreign actors are operating within a common framework. This framework need not be restrictive or definitive. It need not be set in stone right from the beginning. In fact, it must be adaptive and flexible. However, it would also need to be more than a preliminary accord signed at the start of the international engagement. At the very least, this framework would have to take into account not just competing local interests, but also the myriad overlapping interests and preoccupations of a host of international organizations.

NOTES

1. See *The Causes of Conflict and the Promotion of Durable Peace and Sustainable Development in Africa,* Report of the Secretary-General to the United Nations Security Council, April 1998, par. 63 (http://www.un.org/ecosocdev/geninfo/afrec/sgreport/report.htm).

2. Three years after the international intervention, the problem of violence due to popular frustration remained. Christopher Marquis, writing in the *Miami Herald,* quoted William Goodfellow and James Morrell of the Center for International Policy in Washington, D.C., as saying, "The disappointment and anger are palpable. The security threat in Haiti is not from a civil war but a civic explosion." See "Haiti Taxing the Patience of Its Friends," *Miami Herald,* November 27, 1997.

3. Apart from the sources cited in these notes, the conclusions and observations in this paper are drawn from six field trips to Haiti between January 1996 and April 1998; from over a hundred conversations with international policy makers and Haitian leaders during that period; from International Peace Academy Policy Forums on Haiti in March 1996 and July 1997; and a forum involving members of the Haitian diaspora organized by the Advisory Group on Development in Haiti and the International Peace Academy in October 1997.

4. Michel-Rolph Trouillot writes of politics in Haiti in the late nineteenth century: "The Libérals, most of whom were associated with the more Westernized mulâtre elite ... emphasized competence, economic liberalism, and, most of all, the need to limit the power of the Executive. The remainder of the Legislature soon gathered around the Parti National, an even looser organization whose members shared only a vague affinity for the kind of populism embodied by Salnave. To the Libéral leit-motif, 'Power to the most competent,' the Nationals replied, 'The greatest good to the greatest number.'" Trouillot, *Haiti—State Against Nation: The Origins and Legacy of Duvalierism* (New York: Monthly Review Press, 1990), pp. 97–99. The parallels with contemporary Haiti are striking.

5. In this regard, see Anthony Schindler-Hattenbach, *Hot Times in Haiti* (Miami: J.M.S. Publishings, 1994).

6. A sense of this is conveyed by Herbert Gold, "One Step Forward and Two Steps Back, Set to the Haitian Beat," *Washington Post,* February 15, 1998.

7. See Jennifer L. McCoy, "Introduction," in Robert I. Rotberg, ed.,

Haiti Renewed: Political and Economic Prospects (Washington, D.C.: Brookings Institution Press, 1997), p. 9.

8. I would recommend highly that anyone writing on Haiti should spend at least one day trying to drive through the Haitian countryside in order to fully grasp the limitations on what can be known about Haiti.

9. To get a sense of Haiti's lure for foreigners, see Bob Shacochis, "There Must be a God in Haiti," *Outside Magazine,* November 1996. See also Don Bohning, "A Lifelong Love Affair with Haitian Culture," *Miami Herald,* April 21, 1997.

10. See Michael W. Doyle, *UN Peacekeeping in Cambodia: UNTAC's Civil Mandate* (Boulder: Lynne Rienner, 1995, for the International Peace Academy).

11. The increasing vigor of the OAS's commitment to democracy was dramatic: in 1985, the Protocol of Cartagena de Indias incorporated democracy-promotion in the OAS Charter; in 1989 the Organization began to observe elections in member states when requested; in 1990 it created a "Unit for Promotion of Democracy" and launched additional programs to bolster democratization; in 1991 its General Assembly adopted a mechanism to respond when democratic order is interrupted in any member state; and in 1992 it strengthened its several instruments for promoting democratic government in the Protocol of Washington.

12. Resolution 40 / 27B.

13. Resolution 841 (1993).

14. Resolution 861 (1993) lifted the embargo, and Resolution 867 (September 3, 1993) authorized UNMIH.

15. "UN OKs Police Mission in Haiti," *Miami Herald,* December 2, 1997.

16. David Malone, "Haiti and the International Community: A Case Study," *Survival* 39, 2 (Summer 1997), p. 134.

17. Serge F. Kovaleski, "Haitians Find New Police Too Similar to Old," *Washington Post,* July 14, 1997.

18. Don Bohning, "Haiti Police a Gutsy Work in Progress," *Miami Herald,* May 8, 1997.

19. See Michael Norton, "Haiti Pols Lay Blame on Aristide," Associated Press, March 24, 1997.

20. One of the biggest, and newest, threats to Haiti's security at the time of writing was the increasing emergence of Haiti as a transshipment point for cocaine and other drugs to the United States. See Serge F. Kovaleski, "Cartels 'Buying' Haiti," *Washington Post,* February 16, 1998.

21. While reevaluating international efforts in Haiti, a senior international official reportedly stated that if things were to be done over again, security would have to be dealt with only in the context of progress in other critical areas.

22. See Report of the Secretary-General on the United Nations Transition Mission in Haiti, October 31, 1997 (S/1997/832).

23. Don Bohning, "Haiti Persists in Move Toward Business Privatization," *Miami Herald,* July 25, 1997.

24. Don Bohning, "Aristide Comeback? It's Up to the Voters," *Miami Herald,* April 5, 1997. The Famille Lavalas group was one of the two primary groups—the other being the Lavalas Political Organization, or OPL (subsequently renamed the Organisation du Peuple en Lutte)—into which the original Lavalas Movement had split over the issue of Aristide having to make way for Preval.

25. On August 19, 1997, the United Nations suspended electoral assistance to Haiti until the Provisional Electoral Council could establish that it was capable of holding free and fair elections. Michael Norton, "UN Suspends Election Aid in Haiti," Associated Press, August 22, 1997.

26. Michael Norton, "Haitian Drought Brings Famine Threat," *Miami Herald,* May 8, 1997.

27. These conclusions are drawn from first-hand observations of UN peacekeeping in Haiti in January–February 1996, and again in October 1997.

28. Michael Norton, "Opponents Say Aristide's Party Hired Gunmen," *Miami Herald,* April 10, 1997. "Although the United States has declared the weekend election fair, two candidates claim former..."

29. Sidney W. Mintz, "Can Haiti Change?" *Foreign Affairs* 74, 1 (January-February 1995), p. 73.

30. Ibid., p. 74. See also Trouillot, *Haiti,* p. 37.

31. Mintz, "Can Haiti Change?" pp. 75–77.

32. Trouillot, *Haiti,* pp. 44–48.

33. Mintz, "Can Haiti Change?" pp. 82–83.

34. Trouillot, *Haiti,* pp. 49–50.

35. Ibid., Chap. 2, "A Republic for the Merchants."

36. Ibid., pp. 85–87.

37. Madison Smartt Bell provides an evocative account of the horrors of the war in his *All Souls Rising* (London: Penguin, 1995).

38. Trouillot, *Haiti,* pp. 50–58, 64–69.

39. See Mintz, "Can Haiti Change?" pp. 79–82.

40. Ernest H. Preeg, *The Haitian Dilemma: A Case Study in Demographics, Development, and U.S. Foreign Policy* (Washington, D.C.: Center for Strategic and International Studies, 1996), p. 24.

41. The term *maquiladora* refers to the transfer of low-wage assembly components in the manufacturing process to territories without adequate labor regulation in order to reduce the amount of capital that is invested in labor in more unionized or better regulated environments.

42. See Ali Jalali, "Ferghana: Conflict Prevention," Voice of America Background Report, June 11, 1997. Jalali describes a UNDP program designed to address conflict in the Ferghana area of Central Asia through "labor-intensive projects such as agricultural project processing, home based crafts and services lacking in the valley."

43. Trouillot, *Haiti,* Chap. 3, "The Recurring Crisis."

44. Ibid., pp. 128–130.

45. Ibid., pp. 148–152.

46. Mintz, "Can Haiti Change?" p. 84.

47. Trouillot, *Haiti,* p. 158. "For in spite of noiriste propaganda, François Duvalier was quite polite to the mulâtre-dominated Bord de Mer. The official distribution of the f.o.b. coffee prices bears witness to these commercial profits. The peasant-producer share dropped from 67 percent in 1951–1952 to 41 percent in 1966–1967, whereas the share of merchants and speculateurs rose. The Duvalierist state may have frightened individual merchants, but it did not interfere with the structures of the Merchants' Republic."

48. James Ridgeway and Billy Treger, "AIDing and Abetting Mayhem," *Multinational Monitor,* March 1994.

49. Elements of this strategy are outlined in Alex Dupuy, "Free Trade and Underdevelopment in Haiti: The World Bank/USAID Agenda for Social

Change in the Post-Duvalier Era," in Hilbourne A. Watson, ed., *The Caribbean in the Global Political Economy* (Boulder: Lynne Rienner, 1994.)

50. Ibid., p. 100.

51. Several analysts will disagree with this suggestion. See Mats Lundahl, "The Haitian Dilemma Reexamined," in Rotberg, ed., *Haiti Renewed*. While Lundahl's analysis of the dynamics of the decline of Haitian agriculture, which is based in sound theory and empirical evidence, suggests continued decline unless large numbers of peasants either migrate or are employed in other sectors, I would propose that, given the continued insistence of many Haitian agronomists and development workers on the vitality and criticality of the Haitian peasantry, we at least consider the options that still may be available to peasants on the land, rather than thinking first of ways of employing them after they have been pushed off the land. Anthony V. Catanese provides some suggestions in this regard in "Priorities in the Economic Reconstruction of Rural Haiti" in the same volume. For more debate on this issue, see *Aide et Sécurité Alimentaires en Haiti, Forum Libre 21* (Port-au-Prince: Centre Petion Bolivar 1996).

52. Further evidence that overcrowding on land was not the only factor prompting migration is provided by on-site observers. "Camille Chalmers, head of the Haitian Platform for Alternative Development ..., observed, 'We saw with our own eyes the quantity of rice which is rotting in the fields because the peasants don't have money or can't find people to work in the fields. [This] creates the paradox of rice rotting in the fields in a country where there is hunger'" (see "Feeding Dependency ..."; http://www.wohaiti.org).

53. For some explanations for why this did not happen, see Robert Maguire et al., *Haiti Held Hostage: International Responses to the Quest for Nationhood, 1986–1996*, Occasional Paper 23, Thomas J. Watson, Jr., Institute for International Studies and the United Nations University, 1996, p. 25.

54. Economist Alex Dupuy has the following to say: "Though the exports of assembly manufactured goods now surpassed coffee exports in their percentage of total exports, most of the wealth generated from the assembly manufacturing industries was reinvested abroad. Moreover, importing consumer and luxury goods for the consumption of the middle class and the bourgeoisie, and cheap food to substitute for domestic food production deficiencies, resulted in the further draining of the country's wealth and in the increased despoilation of the peasantry." See Alex Dupuy, *Haiti in the World Economy: Class, Race, and Underdevelopment Since 1700* (Boulder: Westview, 1989), p. 209.

55. An important aspect of this problem has been identified by Jean-Germain Gros. Critiquing the current international emphasis on privatization, he says: "The problem in Haiti is not too strong a state and too weak a private sector. Instead, the problem is a weak state, hard put to secure property rights, and an unregulated private sector where the line between entrepreneurship and racketeering is fuzzy, and where those who are engaged in either or both seldom pay taxes." See "Haiti's Flagging Transition," *Journal of Democracy* 8, 4 (October 1997), p. 104.

56. Simon M. Fass, *Political Economy in Haiti: The Drama of Survival* (New Brunswick, N.J.: Transaction, 1990).

57. A Haitian colleague once informed me that even with poor, Creole-language medical training, migrant Haitian doctors in the United States per-

formed better in medical tests than migrants from most other countries. For the most part, they just taught themselves.

58. Although there are exceptions that prove the point. See Dawud Byron, "Caribbean Island Votes to Secede," Associated Press, October 14, 1997. "Once reliant on sugar, cotton, and coconuts for revenue, both islands [St. Kitts and Nevis] depend increasingly on tourism, offshore banking, and light- and high-technology industries for income."

59. For details of the impact of USAID policies in Haiti, and particularly of the pig slaughter, see Paul Farmer, *AIDS and Accusation: Haiti and the Geography of Blame* (Berkeley: University of California Press, 1992).

60. Charles Lane, "Island of Disenchantment: Haiti's Deteriorating Democracy," *The New Republic*, September 29, 1997.

61. Preeg, *The Haitian Dilemma*, p. 19.

62. I witnessed this cooperation first-hand during a drive through the Artibonite Valley in 1997. In the rural community of La Chappelle, local residents had pooled resources to create and sustain an impressively functional school, with teachers, blackboards, desks, and of course, students. When our vehicles broke down on the rugged tracks that pass for roads in Haiti, it proved impressively simple, without first offering large sums of money, to organize members of the local population to provide assistance.

63. Amy Wilentz, *The Rainy Season: Haiti Since Duvalier* (New York: Simon and Schuster, 1989), pp. 89–90.

64. For some of the reforms developed by the first Aristide government, and the reasons for why these reforms challenged the interests of the traditional elite, see Alex Dupuy, *Haiti in the New World Order: The Limits of the Democratic Revolution* (Boulder: Westview, 1997), pp. 115–117.

65. Aristide "'acted quickly to restore order to the government's finances' after taking power 'when the economy was in an unprecedented state of disintegration' (Inter-American Development Bank). Other international lending agencies agreed, offering aid and endorsing Aristide's investment program. They were particularly impressed by the steps he took to reduce foreign debt and inflation, to raise foreign exchange reserves from near zero to $12 million, to increase government revenues with successful tax collection measures (reaching into the kleptocracy), to streamline the bloated government bureaucracy and eliminate fictitious positions in an anti-corruption campaign, to cut back contraband and improve customs, and to establish a responsible fiscal system.... The U.S. embassy in Haiti secretly acknowledged the facts. In a February, 1991, State Department cable, declassified in 1994, the number two person in the Embassy, Vicky Huddleston, reported to Washington on 'the surprisingly successful efforts of the Aristide government ... quickly reversed after the coup.'" Noam Chomsky, "Democracy Enhancement, Part II: The Case of Haiti," *Z Magazine*, July/August 1994.

66. John Canham-Clyne, "The U.S. and Haitian Democracy: Aristide's Human Rights Record," *Peace and Democracy*, Summer 1994.

67. See Robert Fatton, Jr., "The Rise, Fall, and Resurrection of President Aristide," in Rotberg, ed., *Haiti Renewed*, p. 145.

68. A prominent Haitian woman leader graphically recalled these horrors during a 1997 conversation, and attested to the trauma that these violations had created both for the national psyche as well as democracy.

69. See summary of Grassroots International report, "Feeding

Dependency, Starving Democracy: USAID Policies in Haiti," on the website of the Washington Office on Haiti (http://www.wohaiti.org).

70. Ibid.

71. See Bob Shacochis, "Our Hidden Haitian Problem," *The Washington Post* National Weekly Edition, April 8–14, 1996, p. 23. "One after another, alleged criminals from FRAPH and the army, arrested by A-teams and in detention in Port-au-Prince, were inexplicably released within 48 hours, according to the Special Forces team members whom I interviewed." Some officials subsequently argued that there was no option but to release the detainees given the lack of adequate prison facilities. However, since some of the detainees presented a threat to the safety of the U.S. troops and their mission, this was a barely credible explanation. If space were the issue, a triage of sorts could have been carried out among the detainees, with the leaders among the offenders held in temporary facilities and the others released.

72. For an account of some of the operational and tactical challenges faced by the U.S. forces in Haiti, see Margaret Daly Hayes and Gary F. Wheatley, eds., *Interagency and Political-Military Dimensions of Peace Operations: Haiti—A Case Study*, An ACT Workshop Report (Washington, D.C.: National Defense University, 1996).

73. A viable exit policy formed one of the cornerstones of the U.S. Presidential Decision Directive 25, which established the criteria for U.S. involvement in international peace support operations.

74. See Jean Jean-Pierre, "The Tenth Department," in James Ridgeway, ed., *The Haiti Files: Decoding the Crisis* (Washington, D.C.: Essential Books/ Azul Editions, 1994).

75. Several international officials, including some attending an International Peace Academy Forum on Haiti in 1997, have attested informally to the failure of Haiti's experiment with a national truth commission along the lines of South Africa and several Latin American countries.

76. See the discussion of this system in A. K. Majumdar and Bhanwar Singh, eds., *Panchayat Politics and Community Development* (New Delhi: Vedams Books, 1996).

77. So successful was this project in avoiding middlemen that a leading left-wing Haitian agronomist, who had taken strong exception to U.S. policies in Haiti in the past, admitted to me in 1998 that he was willing to revise his opinion of the U.S. ability to learn from its mistakes.

78. Some USAID projects in recent years had begun to show a laudable trend towards more participatory project implementation in Haiti. See Mimi Whitfield, "Clean Water, Garbage Pickup Slated for Cité Soleil Slum," *Miami Herald*, November 3, 1997.

79. Christopher Marquis, "Haitian Coffee Project Stirs Reforestation Hopes," *Miami Herald*, August 16, 1997.

80. The debate over the relevance of assembly manufacturing in the Haitian economy is by no means resolved. Clive Gray presents a persuasive argument for why Haiti's economic renaissance will still need to take place at the hands of assembly manufacturers in "Alternative Models for Haiti's Economic Reconstruction" in Rotberg, ed., *Haiti Renewed*.

81. A Canadian official visiting Haiti in 1997 concurred with me on the possibilities of "eco-tourism."

82. See Trouillot, *Haiti*, p. 210.

83. A land reform program launched in the Artibonite Valley by Haiti's

National Institute for Agrarian Reform (INARA) has been attempting to address land disputes and has reportedly attained some measure of success, because the overall level of violence in the Artibonite has declined considerably. However, the project needs to have a stronger focus on encouraging greater productivity, reinvestment in land, and cooperative farming than on attempting a haphazard redistribution of land parcels to peasants. Since all available land is already being cultivated, and land titles remain in a state of flux, this may promote more conflict in the future. See Kathie Klarreich, "Haiti's Land Handout Only Scratches the Surface of Need," *Christian Science Monitor,* March 26, 1997.

84. Fareed Zakaria, "The Rise of Illiberal Democracy," *Foreign Affairs* (November/December 1997), pp. 22–43.

85. Barrington Moore Jr., *Social Origins of Dictatorship and Democracy* (London: Penguin, 1967).

86. Wilentz, *The Rainy Season,* p. 210.

87. Ibid., p. 237.

88. Ibid., p. 332.

89. Gros makes a similar recommendation by arguing for the convening of a constituent assembly that would include both political and civic actors and that would address both issues of national reconciliation and contentious economic problems such as privatization. See Gros, "Haiti's Flagging Transition," pp. 106–107.

90. At the time of writing, at least two attempts to initiate such a dialogue were being made by the international community. The National Democratic Institute for International Affairs (NDI) was taking a representative group of Haitian civic and political leaders to South Africa in May 1998, to discuss the building of democracy with leading South African officials. Also, the International Peace Academy (IPA) had started a series of consultations, beginning in January 1998, between a balanced group of civic and political leaders aimed at establishing a dialogue of this nature. See Report of the Secretary-General on the United Nations Police Mission in Haiti, February 20, 1998, S/1998/144.

BIBLIOGRAPHY

Bell, Madison Smartt. *All Souls Rising*. London: Penguin Books, 1995.
Bohning, Don. "Aristide Comeback? It's Up to the Voters." *Miami Herald*. April 5, 1997.
———. "A Lifelong Love Affair with Haitian Culture." *Miami Herald*. April 21, 1997.
———. "Haiti Police a Gutsy Work in Progress." *Miami Herald*. May 8, 1997.
———. "Haiti Persists in Move Toward Business Privatization." *Miami Herald*. July 25, 1997.
Byron, Dawud. "Caribbean Island Votes To Secede." Associated Press. October 14, 1997.
Canham-Clyne, John. "The U.S. and Haitian Democracy: Aristide's Human Rights Record." *Peace and Democracy*. Summer 1994.
Catanese, Anthony V. "Priorities in the Economic Reconstruction of Rural Haiti." In Robert I. Rotberg, ed., *Haiti Renewed: Political and Economic Prospects*. Washington, D.C.: Brookings Institution Press, 1997.
Centre Petion Bolivar. *Aide et Sécurité Alimentaires en Haiti*. Forum Libre 21. Port-au-Prince, Haiti, 1996.
Chomsky, Noam. "Democracy Enhancement Part II: The Case of Haiti." *Z Magazine* (July/August 1994).
Christian Science Monitor. Editorial. "The CIA and Haiti." November 2, 1993.
Dobbins, James F. "Haiti: A Case Study in Post–Cold War Peacekeeping." ISD Reports, Vol. II, No. 1. Washington, D.C.: Institute for the Study of Diplomacy, Georgetown University, 1995.
Doyle, Michael W. *UN Peacekeeping in Cambodia: UNTAC's Civil Mandate*. Boulder: Lynne Rienner, for the International Peace Academy, 1995.
Dupuy, Alex. "Free Trade and Underdevelopment in Haiti: The World Bank/USAID Agenda for Social Change in the Post-Duvalier Era." In Hilbourne A. Watson, ed., *The Caribbean in the Global Political Economy*. Boulder: Lynne Rienner, 1994.
———. *Haiti in the World Economy: Class, Race, and Underdevelopment Since 1700*. Boulder: Westview, 1989.
———. *Haiti in the New World Order: The Limits of the Democratic Revolution*. Boulder: Westview, 1997.
Farmer, Paul. *AIDS and Accusation: Haiti and the Geography of Blame*. Berkeley: University of California Press, 1992.

Fass, Simon M. *Political Economy in Haiti: The Drama of Survival.* New Brunswick, N.J.: Transaction, 1990.

Fatton, Robert, Jr. "The Rise, Fall, and Resurrection of President Aristide." In Robert I. Rotberg, ed., *Haiti Renewed: Political and Economic Prospects.* Washington, D.C.: Brookings Institution Press, 1997.

Gold, Herbert. "One Step Forward and Two Steps Back, Set to the Haitian Beat." *Washington Post.* February 15, 1998.

Grassroots International. *Feeding Dependency, Starving Democracy: USAID Policies in Haiti* (summary of report). http://www.wohaiti.org.

Gray, Clive. "Alternative Models for Haiti's Economic Reconstruction." In Robert I. Rotberg, ed., *Haiti Renewed: Political and Economic Prospects.* Washington, D.C.: Brookings Institution Press, 1997.

Gros, Jean-Germain. "Haiti's Flagging Transition." *Journal of Democracy* 8, 4 (October 1997).

Hayes, Margaret Daly, and Gary F. Wheatley, eds. *Interagency and Political-Military Dimensions of Peace Operations: Haiti—A Case Study,* An ACT workshop report. Washington, D.C.: National Defense University, 1996.

Human Rights Watch / Americas, National Coalition for Haitian Rights, Washington Office on Latin America. "Haiti: The Human Rights Record of the Haitian National Police." *Human Rights Watch Reports.* Vol. 9, No. 1(B). January 1997.

Jalali, Ali. "Ferghana/Conflict Prevention." Voice of America Background Report. June 11, 1997.

Jean-Pierre, Jean. "The Tenth Department." In James Ridgeway, ed., *The Haiti Files: Decoding the Crisis.* Washington, D.C.: Essential Books / Azul Editions, 1994.

Klarreich, Kathie. "Haiti's Land Handout Only Scratches the Surface of Need." *Christian Science Monitor.* March 26, 1997.

Kovaleski, Serge F. "Haitians Find New Police Too Similar to Old." *Washington Post.* July 14, 1997.

———. "Cartels 'Buying' Haiti." *Washington Post.* February 16, 1998.

Kumar, Chetan, and Elizabeth Cousens. "Peacebuilding in Haiti." Policy Briefing Series. New York: International Peace Academy, 1996.

Lane, Charles. "Island of Disenchantment: Haiti's Deteriorating Democracy." *New Republic.* September 29, 1997.

Lundahl, Mats. "The Haitian Dilemma Reexamined." In Robert I. Rotberg, ed., *Haiti Renewed: Political and Economic Prospects.* Washington, D.C.: Brookings Institution Press, 1997.

Maguire, Robert, et al. *Haiti Held Hostage: International Responses to the Quest for Nationhood, 1986–96.* Occasional Paper 23, Thomas J. Watson Jr. Institute for International Studies and the United Nations University, 1996.

Malone, David. "Haiti and the International Community: A Case Study." *Survival* 39, 2 (Summer 1997).

Marks, Alexandra. "Haitian Military's Drug and CIA Ties: Panama Reprise?" *Christian Science Monitor.* November 3, 1993.

———. "Haiti Still Stymies Clinton as Military Defies the UN: Administration Policy Blasted by Critics on Both the Left and the Right." *Christian Science Monitor.* November 15, 1993.

Marquis, Christopher. "Haitian Coffee Project Stirs Reforestation Hopes." *Miami Herald.* August 16, 1997.

———. "Haiti Taxing the Patience of Its Friends." *Miami Herald.* November 27, 1997.

McCoy, Jennifer L. "Introduction," in Robert I. Rotberg, ed., *Haiti Renewed: Political and Economic Prospects.* Washington, D.C.: Brookings Institution Press, 1997.

McGeary, Johanna. "Does the American Mission Matter?" *Time.* February 19, 1996.

Miami Herald. "UN OKs Police Mission in Haiti." Wire Services, December 2, 1997.

Mintz, Sidney W. "Can Haiti Change?" *Foreign Affairs* 74, 1 (January/February 1995).

Moore, Barrington, Jr. *Social Origins of Dictatorship and Democracy.* London: Penguin, 1967.

Norton, Michael. "Haiti Polls Lay Blame on Aristide." Associated Press. March 24, 1997.

———. "UN Suspends Election Aid in Haiti." Associated Press. August 22, 1997.

———. "Haitian Drought Brings Famine Threat." Associated Press/*Miami Herald.* May 8, 1997.

———. "Opponents Say Aristide's Party Hired Gunmen." *Miami Herald.* April 10, 1997.

Oakley, Robert, and Michael Dziedzic. "Sustaining Success in Haiti..." Strategic Forum No. 77. Washington D.C.: Institute for National Strategic Studies, National Defense University, June 1996.

O'Neill, William G. "Human Rights Monitoring vs. Political Expediency: The Experience of the OAS/UN Mission in Haiti." *Harvard Human Rights Journal.* Vol. 8, Spring 1995.

Pouliot, J.O.G. (Neil), Chief Superintendent (retd) RCMP. "The Role and Functions of Civilian Police in United Nations Peacekeeping Operations: The Haitian Experience." Paper presented to the International Peace Academy Seminar on Peacemaking and Peacekeeping. Vienna, Austria, June 14–25, 1996.

Preeg, Ernest H. *The Haitian Dilemma: A Case Study in Demographics, Development, and U.S. Foreign Policy.* Washington, D.C.: Center for Strategic and International Studies, 1996.

Press, Eyal. "Obstructing Justice in Haiti." *Christian Science Monitor.* November 8, 1997.

Ridgeway, James, and Treger, Billy. "AIDing and Abetting Mayhem." *Multinational Monitor* (March 1994).

Rohter, Larry. "Haitian Accused of Rights Abuses Is Freed by the US." *New York Times.* June 22, 1996.

Roumain, Jacques. *Masters of the Dew.* Oxford: Heinemann, 1998.

Schindler-Hattenbach, Anthony. *Hot Times in Haiti.* Miami: J.M.S. Publishings, 1994.

Shacochis, Bob. "There Must Be a God in Haiti." *Outside Magazine* (November 1996).

———. "Our Hidden Haitian Problem." *Washington Post* National Weekly Edition. April 8–14, 1996, p. 23.

Trouillot, Michel-Rolph. *Haiti–State Against Nation: The Origins and Legacy of Duvalierism.* New York: Monthly Review Press, 1990.

Whitfield, Mimi. "Clean Water, Garbage Pickup Slated for Cité Soleil Slum." *Miami Herald.* November 3, 1997.

Wilentz, Amy. *The Rainy Season: Haiti Since Duvalier.* New York: Simon and Schuster, 1989.

Zakaria, Fareed. "The Rise of Illiberal Democracy." *Foreign Affairs* (November/December 1997), pp. 22–43.

UN DOCUMENTS

Security Council Resolution S/RES/40/ 27B.

Security Council Resolution S/RES/841 (1993).

Security Council Resolution S/RES/861 (1993).

Security Council Resolution S/RES/867. September 3, 1993.

Report of the Secretary-General on the United Nations Transition Mission in Haiti, S/1997/832, October 31, 1997.

Report of the Secretary-General on the United Nations Police Mission in Haiti, S/1998/144, February 20, 1998.

United Nations Security Council. *The Causes of Conflict and the Promotion of Durable Peace and Sustainable Development in Africa,* Report of the Secretary-General to the United Nations Security Council, April 1998. (HYPERLINK http://www.un.org/ecosocdev/geninfo/afrec/sgreport/report.htm.)

ABOUT THIS OCCASIONAL PAPER

Though its national life often has been characterized by violence, Haiti has not been victim of a full-fledged internal conflict, or civil war. Why, then, is the international community conducting "postconflict peacebuilding" operations there? Addressing that question, Chetan Kumar examines the course of international involvement in Haiti through the prism of the country's unique past and present. His narrative is grounded in a discussion of the nature of peacebuilding and the role of civil society in building a functioning state.

A basket of nonmilitary activities designed to address some of the primary causes of violence—weak institutions, underdevelopment, and poverty—have come to be referred to as postconflict peacebuilding in the Haitian context. How do these activities differ from the numerous development schemes launched from the mid-1960s onward? Is peacebuilding essentially about successful development? Kumar engages the recent heated debate about these issues.

Haitians have struggled among themselves to define the nature, structure, and power base of a state that can best provide for its constituents—and their conception frequently is at odds with the one promoted by the international community. Building a lasting peace, Kumar emphasizes, will be possible only if Haitians themselves support any given understanding of what a successful polity and economy should look like, and if they participate in bringing it about. He concludes with recommendations aimed at encouraging that participation.

Chetan Kumar is senior associate at the International Peace Academy (IPA) and director of the IPA Project on Policy Advocacy and Facilitation in Haiti. Previously he was research associate at the University of Illinois Program in Arms Control, Disarmament, and

International Security. He is coeditor (with Marvin Weinbaum) of *South Asia Approaches the Millennium: Reexamining National Security,* and author (with Elizabeth Cousens) of "Peacebuilding in Haiti," IPA Policy Briefing (April 1996).

THE INTERNATIONAL PEACE ACADEMY

The International Peace Academy is an independent, nonpartisan, international institution devoted to the promotion of peaceful and multilateral approaches to the resolution of international as well as internal conflicts. IPA plays a facilitating role in efforts to settle conflicts, providing a middle ground where the options for settling particular conflicts are explored and promoted in an informal setting. Other activities of the organization include public forums; training seminars on conflict resolution and peacekeeping; and research and workshops on collective security, regional and internal conflicts, peacemaking, peacekeeping, and nonmilitary aspects of security.

In fulfilling its mission, IPA works closely with the United Nations, regional and other international organizations, governments, and parties to conflicts. The work of IPA is further enhanced by its ability to draw on a worldwide network of eminent persons comprising government leaders, statesmen, business leaders, diplomats, military officers, and scholars. In the decade following the end of the Cold War, there has been a general awakening to the enormous potential of peaceful and multilateral approaches to resolving conflicts. This has given renewed impetus to the role of IPA.

IPA is governed by an international board of directors. Financial support for the work of the organization is provided primarily by philanthropic foundations, as well as individual donors.

OTHER INTERNATIONAL PEACE ACADEMY

PUBLICATIONS

Available from Lynne Rienner Publishers, 1800 30th Street, Boulder, Colorado 80301 (303-444-6684):

The United Nations in a Turbulent World, James N. Rousenau
United Nations Peacekeeping and the Non-Use of Force, F. T. Liu
The Wave of the Future: The United Nations and Naval Peacekeeping, Robert Stephens Staley II
Political Order in Post-Communist Afghanistan, William Maley and Fazel Haq Saikal
Seeking Peace from Chaos: Humanitarian Intervention in Somalia, Samuel M. Makinda
Aftermath of the Gulf War: An Assessment of UN Action, Ian Johnstone
Presiding Over a Divided World: Changing UN Roles, 1945–1993, Adam Roberts and Benedict Kingsbury
UN Peacekeeping in Cambodia, Michael W. Doyle
Rights and Reconciliation: UN Strategies in El Salvador, Ian Johnstone